How to PLAN for
LONG-TERM CARE

FREE Online Assessment

Protect Your Family and Your Legacy:
Create a *Smart LTC Plan*™

ALLEN HAMM

Plan NOW for Long-Term Care:
Protect Your Family, Secure Your Legacy

Without a written plan for long-term care, our family will be forced to make painful and sometimes urgent decisions—decisions about the type of care we may need, who will provide our care, where care will be provided, and who will pay for it.

———————◆———————

If I Knew Then What I Know Now

"My mother, Millie, passed away a couple of months ago at 92 after a 12-year battle with Alzheimer's disease. Although she had been very astute in planning for her financial security, there was no way she or my sisters and I could have anticipated what the financial and emotional toll of caring for her would be. If I knew then what I know now, I would have hoped for the best but planned for the worst."

— *Megan Martin*

———————◆———————

A Family Affair

"When my wife and I moved my in-laws from the home they had lived in for 40 years, my father-in-law said to me, 'I sure wish we had planned for this.' He was worried that all their hard-earned savings, accumulated over a lifetime, would be used to pay for care. Both of them ended up dying in a nursing home, having used all but $2,000 of their estate."

— *Don Olson*

———————◆———————

Our Promise

"It was a promise all five children made to our mother—we would never put her in a nursing home. Mom was diagnosed with Alzheimer's when she was 85. Our normally fit and healthy mother was now frail and confused. Three of us are now taking turns having her live with us for three to four months at a time. If we hadn't planned ahead, we would never have been able to afford the supplemental assistance needed to care for her."

— *Michelle LaMarche*

How to PLAN for
LONG-TERM CARE

Protect Your Family and Your Legacy:
Create a *Smart LTC Plan*™

ALLEN HAMM

ISBN: 0-9764189-5-9

Published by:	Plan Ahead, Inc.
Editor:	Annamarie O'Shea
Graphic Design:	Quin Coursey, QuinCoursey@comcast.net
Interior Photos:	©PhotoDisc/Getty Images ©Dynamic Graphics, ©Banana Stock

Dedication

Dedicated to my wife Eileen, and to my two sons, Brian and Alex.

Acknowledgments

This book exists because of the encouragement of my wife, Eileen. Throughout the entire project, she reinforced the importance of getting this information into the hands of American families. She also contributed her personal perspectives throughout and completely wrote *Chapter 5: Why Is Long-Term Care a Women's Issue?*

Thanks to Estate Planning Attorney Julie Fiedler for explaining in layman's terms the technical aspects of Medicaid in *Chapter 4.*

Thanks to the *Objective Financial Advisors* (see page 59) who assisted with the 7 step *Smart LTC Planning*™ process explained in Chapter 7.

Thanks to Annamarie O'Shea for her total commitment to editing and managing this project while still handling all her usual duties.

Thanks to Quin Coursey for her graphic design services, helping us elevate an often boring and negative topic to a more engaging level.

TABLE OF CONTENTS

One Page Book Summary

I know long-term care is a dull and negative subject. I've tried making this book as interesting as possible, but for those who never get around to reading it...here are the major points you don't want to miss. If you only have 2 minutes to spend on this book, please read this page.

For those of you who want definitions, descriptions, examples, and more, dive into Part One.

What you need to know about Long-Term Care

➤ LTC is defined as the need for assistance with the normal activities of daily living for a period of greater than 100 days. Short-term care is of little concern.

➤ There is usually a "continuum of long-term care" that starts at home, then may advance to an assisted living community, and as a last resort, or at the end of life, a nursing home.

➤ Long-term care is expensive and is one of the greatest risks to your financial security.

➤ There are only 4 options for paying for long-term care:
   1. Family
   2. Medicaid (Welfare)
   3. Personal Assets
   4. LTC insurance

➤ Regular Health Insurance and Medicare **DO NOT** cover LTC expenses.

➤ LTC is a women's issue – they are the majority of caregivers as well as the largest group requiring LTC services for the longest period of time.

What you need to know about planning for Long-Term Care

➤ Your LTC Plan **MUST** be integrated with your financial and estate objectives.

➤ **DO NOT** rely on the services of a financial professional or insurance agent who uses a non-integrative approach of simply trying to sell you insurance.

➤ Online tools available at **www.smartltcplan.com** can help you develop your own personal plan for paying for long-term care.

➤ After going through the *Smart LTC Planning*™ process at the above url, request a meeting with an *Objective Financial Advisor* (see page 59).

Still have 10 minutes to spare? Read the "Key Points" at the end of each chapter.

PREFACE
Long-Term Care Is America's
True Health Care Crisis

In the coming decades, the healthy lifestyles that will enable millions of Americans to live well beyond age 100 may also pose the greatest threat to their financial security, retirement, and legacy. Our biggest challenge in the field of health care will be to physically and psychologically care for those who have managed to live well beyond today's life expectancy.

It has been estimated that the number of people requiring long-term care will double in the next three decades. This means that more than 28 million people could need help with the basic activities of daily living, or some level of supervision due to memory loss. Tasks such as getting dressed, which are now performed with ease by most, will require the assistance of others. Unable to live independently, these large numbers of people requiring care will create tremendous demand for new health care solutions in the first half of the twenty-first century. This new challenge—accommodating those needing long-term care—will dwarf our current problems regarding the financing of physician and hospital care.

Who will provide this care? Where will the care take place? Who will pay the bills? The long-term care industry is working to find the answers to many of these questions. Soon, planning ahead for long-term care will become as common as creating a will.

One option for paying for care is long-term care insurance. We devote several chapters of this book to a discussion of this option. If you haven't already purchased long-term care insurance, we encourage you to wait the few hours it will take to read this book. After doing so, you should then consult with an *Objective Financial Advisor* (see page 59)—rather than an insurance agent. An advisor will assist you in planning ahead for long-term care by guiding you to resources and information that help you understand your options within the context of your personal and financial objectives.

Attempting to plan ahead for long-term care outside the context of your financial objectives is a major mistake made by many people. Why? Because the LTC Planning industry is heavily influenced by the insurance industry. Traditional insurance agents often use a *non-integrated approach*, attempting to convince you that long-term care insurance is the only option available for paying for long-term care. The critical difference between working with an *Objective Financial Advisor* and working solely with an insurance agent can mean the difference between success and failure for your financial and estate plan, as well as for your legacy.

To help you create your **Smart LTC Plan**™, an online assessment is available free of charge to readers of this book. For access, go to **www.smartltcplan.com.**

INTRODUCTION

In my 24 years of LTC Planning experience, I have heard hundreds of painful stories about the effects of long-term care. The following story recounts my personal experiences in this area. My purpose in sharing these experiences with you is to communicate the foundation for my strong belief in planning ahead for long-term care.

For those anxious to learn about the specifics of planning ahead, I invite you to move ahead to **Part 1: Understanding Long-Term Care.**

MY FAMILY'S EXPERIENCE WITH LONG-TERM CARE

*I pondered my family's lack of knowledge
about long-term care planning. How could
we know so much about most financial issues
but know so little about such a critical part
of the financial and estate planning process?*

— Allen Hamm

My family has confronted long-term care twice in two separate generations. These experiences were turning points in my life. They influenced my decision to create a process for integrating long-term care planning with financial and estate planning, and they motivated me to help others by writing this book.

I was raised in a traditional American family. Growing up, I dreamed of owning my own business, and maybe even buying the small company my grandfather owned. He had built a successful business that supported many of his family members for several decades.

By the late 1970s, when my grandfather was 72, we began to notice a slight change in his mental alertness. Since he appeared to be managing the company without any problems, we paid little attention to it at first. But we began to take it seriously when we received complaints from his suppliers about late invoice payments. Then, one day, we got a call from a close family friend who owned one of the businesses that supplied his materials. "Allen," he said, "your grandfather's check just bounced." There was shock in his voice and a dead silence on my end of the phone. My grandfather had always been meticulous about keeping his accounts organized.

Over the next few months, my family was subjected to a painful series of discoveries about the state of my grandfather's mental health and his company's finances. We learned that he was suffering from early-onset Alzheimer's disease. The condition was causing him to slowly lose control of both his personal life and his business affairs. By the time we discovered the true depth of his problems, it was too late. His once thriving company was in financial trouble.

Within two years of his diagnosis, my grandfather required a level of long-term care our family could no longer provide at home. We contacted Medicare, expecting that as a hardworking American businessman who had made a positive contribution to society and the economy, he would be well covered for whatever medical and custodial care services he might require. What we learned was almost as upsetting as our original discoveries: Neither his Medicare nor his Medicare Supplement policy offered coverage for long-term custodial care. And although he had lost most of his assets in the demise of his business, he still had too much money to qualify for Medicaid, the welfare program.

Prior to my grandfather's health problems, my parents had been diligently saving for retirement. But after my grandfather's mental and financial decline, they were forced to cash in their savings to fund quality care for my grandfather. He spent the last four years of his life in a private pay nursing home.

After the loss of my grandfather's business, I pondered my family's lack of knowledge about long-term care planning. How could we know so much about most financial issues but know so little about such a critical part of the financial and estate planning process? I became intensely interested in how our country funds the growing demand for the care of people with a need for long-term care.

In the mid-1980s, I moved to California—something I had been considering for several years. Moving 2,000 miles away from my family was one of the most difficult decisions I've ever made. Dad had always been my mentor. Strong, wise, and patient, he had always been able to say or do just the right thing at the right moment. He had never been wealthy, but he instilled in us family values and taught us the importance of planning for our financial future. As an adult, I admired his positive attitude and tenacity, especially after he had experienced adversity and setbacks. Through hard work and integrity, he built a separate company of his own. Inspired by his example and the tragedy that long-term care brought to my grandfather's last years, I fulfilled my own dream of starting a business—one that specializes in assisting people with planning ahead for long-term care *before* the need arises.

After becoming a specialist in long-term care planning, I worked with my parents' financial advisor to evaluate options that would be suitable for their situation. After experiencing my grandfather's long-term care situation, I didn't expect my parents to react enthusiastically to a conversation about their own potential need for long-term care. Few parents want to talk with their children about the possibility of becoming dependent on someone else or requiring assistance with their physical care. However, we all agreed that it made sense to put plans in place that would give them choices we didn't have with my grandfather—plans that would protect the assets they had worked so hard to rebuild after providing for his care. I returned to California pleasantly surprised that they had agreed to plan ahead with no resistance.

About three years later, my father was diagnosed with mild Parkinson's disease. The prognosis was progressive neurological deterioration and, over a period of years, severe physical and cognitive disabilities could be expected. But in the short term, he remained active with his family, business, and church. Our hopes were high that a cure for Parkinson's disease would be found within his lifetime.

Busy with my own family and running our business, I tried to keep a close eye on Dad's condition with frequent phone calls from 2,000 miles away. Fortunately, my brother lives in the same area as my parents and is also able to keep me updated on Dad's physical and mental health.

Shortly before Dad turned 70, my wife, two sons and I attended an eagerly anticipated family reunion. Seeing him for the first time in almost a year, I noticed Dad seemed unusually tired and melancholy. Even his grandsons failed to spark his usual enthusiasm. Concerned about him, I suggested the two of us have a private talk in the backyard. We sat down at an old picnic table where we'd had many family cookouts and private talks. I asked him to open up to me.

His eyes began to water, something I'd never seen. He's a warm person but has always been very much in control of his emotions. He looked away and began to talk.

"Your mom doesn't know, and I don't know how to tell her. Or even you. But here goes…I'm in debt. We're on the verge of losing everything. We're behind on our house payment and the rental property mortgages. The banks are no longer willing to finance our projects. When I was diagnosed with Parkinson's, I knew that I only had a short period of time to get your mother set up, to make sure she wouldn't have to worry once the Parkinson's took control. I rushed with some major business decisions, I made some missteps, and I took on too many projects. I've lost control of where we are financially."

At first, I couldn't accept what he was telling me. I tried to reassure him, the way he had always reassured me. We were in the family backyard at our familiar picnic table, but I felt as disconnected as if I were watching a movie or having a bad dream. I felt a certain level of panic followed by—I'm ashamed to say—a sense of betrayal. Could this be my mentor, the man I had always looked up to, allowing something to get so out of control? And how could my family repeat something so shockingly similar to what we had been through years earlier with my grandfather?

It was a heartbreaking moment magnified by the realization and the fear of what could happen to any of us, myself included In the midst of all those overwhelming emotions, I didn't find as much comfort as I had expected in knowing that he had a plan for paying for long-term care. Even though we would be spared the financial consequences of a future long-term care need, I realized for a second time that the worst part of this issue called "aging" is the emotional side—watching how it humbles the people we love and how it often affects their ability to remain as emotionally and mentally strong as they had been.

Several years have passed since that afternoon when I once again learned how fast life can change. Fortunately, these past few years have been good to our family; the progression of my dad's Parkinson's has slowed, and after developing a plan of action as a family, the worst of his financial problems have been resolved, although the family home did have to be sold. The last time we visited him, he seemed like his old self again. Naturally, I still worry about the way Parkinson's will affect his future, but we feel very blessed that he is still able to live an independent and productive life.

These types of challenges will continue to affect families in the coming decades as we learn to respond to the ever-growing problem of this new health care crisis called long-term care.

Note: My dad and other family members gave their approval to share this personal story.

Postscript: This introduction was written for the first edition. My dad passed away peacefully at home on September 15, 2011.

PART 1 *Understanding Long-Term Care*

*Education gives you the
clarity to believe only half of what
you hear. Experience gives you the
power to know which half.*

— Jerome Perryman
(paraphrased)

PART 1:
Understanding Long-Term Care

Some of the reluctance to plan ahead for long-term care is due to the general confusion and misinformation surrounding the issue. Some of us fail to plan because of fear of the future; others don't plan because they get poor advice from well meaning friends or so-called "experts."

It is easier to address other aspects of financial and estate planning because the issues are black and white. For instance, we know we need to plan for the effect our death will have on our family. But what about planning for chronic illness and frailty? These issues are almost always accompanied by denial, anger, and fear.

Thinking ahead to a time when we might no longer function independently *is* depressing, but planning for long-term care is imperative. Without a written plan, our families will be forced to make painful and sometimes urgent decisions—decisions about the type of care we need, who will provide the care, where the care will be provided, and who will pay for the care.

Planning ahead means not waiting until a need for long-term care arises to make provisions for an individual's care. Planning now allows us to focus on *emotionally* supporting our loved ones if they ever need care in the future.

Part 1 addresses these key issues and provides you with a foundation for understanding long-term care.

Chapter 1 **What Is Long-Term Care?**

Long-term custodial care for the chronically ill may prove to be the most challenging and expensive of the several demographic time bombs America faces.

— Stephen Moses
President, Center for Long-Term Care Reform, Inc.

Long-term care, in its broadest sense, is defined as a need for assistance with the normal activities of daily living. Long-term care can be required due to a disability or impairment, whether it be physical or mental in nature. We define *true* long-term care as care needed for a period of *greater than 100 days*. We define short-term care as care needed for a period of *less than 100 days*.

Various definitions of long-term care are scattered throughout the industry. For example, insurance agents may attempt to scare you into believing that care needed for less than 100 days is a serious financial risk. This can result in a focus on "small dollars," with too little emphasis placed on the risk of "large dollars" required for true long-term care. Short-term care is financially and emotionally inconvenient; long-term care is financially and emotionally devastating. The problem we need to focus on is **long-term care.**

ACTIVITIES OF DAILY LIVING

The first part of our long-term care definition states that a person needs "assistance." Whether or not a person needs assistance is determined in a variety of ways. Usually, a person's ability to perform basic "activities of daily living" is assessed in order to determine if a need for care exists. Activities of daily living, commonly called *ADLs,* include functions most of us perform daily, including activities such as eating, bathing, dressing, and toileting. Performing ADLs can be broadly defined as "the normal management of daily life without causing harm to oneself or others." Chronic difficulty with performing two or more ADLs independently is the common definition of "needing assistance."

Incidental Activities of Daily Living

Another relevant term is "incidental activities of daily living," also known as *IADLs.* Examples of IADLs include cooking, cleaning, and running errands. While ADL is a medical term used to describe and determine the need for assistance,

FAST FACTS:

- "Baby Boomers" refers to the largest generation in history and includes those born between 1946 and 1964.

- Individuals born dur-ing the baby boom generation began turning 65 in 2011.

- In the next few years, older people will outnumber younger people for the first time in history.

- Care for adults is on the verge of replacing child care as the number one depen-dent care issue.

- The over-85 age group is expected to triple as a percentage of the population by 2050.

- Many people will need care for the last two decades or more of their life.

IADL is a term used to describe and determine the *convenience* services required as a result of ADL loss or impairment.

MENTAL IMPAIRMENT

The need for assistance may also be due to mental impairment. Care due to memory loss, including conditions such as Alzheimer's disease, is up by 10% in the last 5 years.

THE NEED FOR LONG-TERM CARE IS GROWING

The number of people needing long-term care is growing fast and will continue to escalate over the next three decades. Three major trends that gain momentum as each year passes will have a phenomenal impact on health care in general, and long-term care in particular:

1. **You will likely live a long life.** "The Aging of America" is driven by the largest generation in history, the baby boomers. The sheer number—76 million Americans born between 1946 and 1964—has had a significant impact on modern society at every social and economic level. Individuals in this generation began to turn 65 in 2011. The implications of this are profound because the odds of needing true long-term care begin to significantly increase in the years after age 65.

2. **Living a long life will probably result in the need for long-term care prior to one's death.** Our aging population is not only sizable, but also contains many health conscious individuals. A healthy diet and regular exercise have a positive effect on longevity. But our bodies and minds will still eventually wear out, only at a much slower pace.

Medical breakthroughs may contribute to making living to age 100 a common occurrence. Some experts predict that life expectancy could be pushed to 120 years, and possibly beyond. Ironically, many health conscious people will need care for the last two decades or more of their lives.

3. **It is unlikely your family will be able to provide your care.** Adult care is on the verge of replacing child care as the number one dependent care issue. Older people will soon outnumber younger people for the first time in history.

In the past, when a family member needed long-term care, other family members stepped in to fill the role of caregiver. It was usually women, including wives and daughters, who became the primary caregivers for immediate and extended family members.

But the changing family structure is having a profound effect on our ability to assist one another. With more women entering the workforce and careers geographically separating many families, *paid* caregivers will soon provide the bulk of long-term care services.

Cost and Availability of Quality Services

The increase in the number of people needing care will have a profound effect on the cost and availability of care-related services, and the availability of *quality* services is likely to be proportionate to our ability to pay for care. For this reason, long-term care services paid for with private funds—either personal assets or LTC insurance—will provide access to higher quality care.

WHEN DO PEOPLE NEED LONG-TERM CARE?

Although we normally think of long-term care as a concern reserved for the elderly, the need for long-term care can arise at any age. Most of us are aware of younger people who have needed care, usually due to an accident or a disabling illness.

Middle-aged people can also suddenly lose the ability to care for themselves. In mid-life, a need for long-term care usually results from conditions like heart disease or stroke. Mental health conditions also become more prevalent during middle age.

But the reality is that the odds of needing long-term care and the duration of the need for long-term care services begin to increase drastically as we age. The vast majority of people needing care for five years or longer fall into the 65 and older age group.

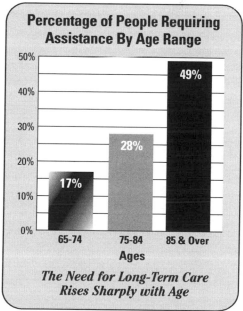

The Need for Long-Term Care Rises Sharply with Age

The most dramatic leap in the need for long-term care comes in the over-85 age group. Almost half of all people over 85 require some form of care, either at home or in a facility. Long-term care is a serious societal issue because this age group is the fastest growing segment of the American population. The over-85 age group will triple as a percentage of the population by 2050.

WHAT ARE THE ODDS OF NEEDING LONG-TERM CARE?

Most available statistics regarding the odds of needing long-term care are misleading because they often include care needed for short periods of time.

One reliable, yet incomplete statistic comes from a recent study by the U.S. Department of Health and Human Services. The study reveals that of all people turning 65 this year, one in four will spend one year or longer in a nursing home. One in eleven will spend five years or longer in a nursing home.

But this statistic does not account for those who need care at home or in an assisted living facility. When the environments of home care and assisted living are factored in, it is estimated there is a 32% chance of needing *true* long-term care during the average person's lifetime.

But what really matters is your ***personal*** odds of needing care. Our online assessment can help you with analyzing that. It takes into consideration such factors as:

- Alzheimer's disease or other forms of dementia in your family: Memory loss is not only the number one cause of needing long-term care, but also the most costly.
- Neurological conditions in your family: Parkinson's disease and other neurological disorders are a common reason for needing long-term care.
- Longevity in your family: A long life expectancy may indicate higher odds of needing care.

CAN YOU REDUCE YOUR ODDS OF NEEDING CARE?

Most people who plan for their future take a proactive approach toward maintaining their health. Ironically, this approach may lead to longevity and raise the odds of needing care in our later years, and for longer periods of time. Still it pays to do all we can to reduce our odds of needing care including:

- **Staying physically active.** Even a minimum level of daily physical activity makes a significant difference.
- **Socializing.** Spend as much time as possible with family and friends. Become involved in activities that include others.

- **Eating with others.** Research has shown that having meals with other people offers multiple benefits. For example, people who eat together are more likely to eat more nutritious meals, which can help them avoid both mental and physical problems. Eating together also offers the opportunity to socialize.

- **Continuously learning.** Challenge your mind daily. Working on crossword puzzles, reading, and stretching your imagination can contribute to a healthier state of mind, potentially reducing the odds of needing care due to mental problems like memory loss.

KEY POINTS

What Is Long-Term Care?

➤ A person who needs long-term care requires assistance for an extended period of time—100 days or longer—with little chance of recovery.

➤ A person who needs short-term care requires assistance for a limited period of time—less than 100 days—with an expected outcome of full recovery.

➤ The need for long-term care is growing due to the aging of America, advances in medical science, and changes in the family structure.

➤ The need for long-term care can arise at younger ages due to an accident or disabling illness.

➤ The fastest growing segment of our population is the over-85 age group. Almost half of all people in this age group require some form of long-term care.

➤ Your individual odds of needing long-term care can be analyzed at **www.smartltcplan.com.**

Chapter 2
Where Is Long-Term Care Received?

It's nice to be here. At my age it's nice to be anywhere.
— George Burns

A person in need of long-term care can be cared for in a variety of settings, including their home, an assisted living community, or a nursing home. The severity of the condition and the level of care required will dictate the environment in which a person's care can be safely and adequately received.

The ultimate goal of any type of care is to help an individual maintain comfort and, if possible, regain some or all of their ability to live independently.

LEVELS OF CARE

There are two broad levels of long-term care: *skilled* and *non-skilled.*

Skilled Care

Someone with an *acute condition* that requires intensive medical attention will normally require a short period of skilled care.

This type of care would likely fall into the category of *short-term care* because the duration of the need for care is almost always less than 100 days.

The two objectives of skilled care are:

- Assist the person and provide them with comfort if the condition is terminal. This type of care is often referred to as *hospice care.*

or

- Assist the person during a recovery period.

Skilled care is sometimes covered by public and private health insurance programs and by Medicare. For example, we knew the owner of a window cleaning company who fell off a roof one morning and broke just about every bone in his body. The prognosis given by his physician was full recovery. He did fully recuperate, and his health insurance paid his medical expenses until he was back on his feet. He even went into a nursing home for two weeks to receive skilled care. The expenses were covered by his health insurance because he required care for only a short period of time and was expected to fully recover from his injuries.

Non-Skilled Care

Most people in need of care receive non-skilled care, frequently called *custodial care.* This level of care is administered to a person who has a *chronic condition,*

FAST FACTS:

- **57%** of all people with a disability rely exclusively on unpaid care from family members or other informal caregivers at home.

- Home care is projected to increase by **178%** by 2030.

- Elderly patients who spend longer than two years in a nursing home rarely return to their own home.

- There was a **61%** increase in the number of assisted living communities built between 1998 and 2011.

- Alzheimer's disease currently afflicts about four million Americans; this figure is projected to grow by **75%** by 2025.

meaning they will not recover. Custodial care is most commonly received at home or in assisted living communities. Conditions such as Parkinson's disease and Alzheimer's disease, or simply the aging process, can cause a need for custodial care. A disabling accident could also result in the need for non-skilled care, especially in the younger population. Non-skilled care normally lasts for a period of 100 days to several years—the *true* definition of long-term care. Unlike short-term care received for a condition from which a person will recuperate, custodial care is not covered by regular health insurance or Medicare.

THE CONTINUUM OF LONG-TERM CARE

Most people mistakenly assume "long-term care" is synonymous with "nursing home care." In reality, a person's care normally progresses through a continuum of care that rarely requires nursing home confinement. For example, older people experiencing the frailties of aging may first require only a minimal amount of assistance in their home for a few hours each week. If the condition worsens and they experience problems with maintaining their balance, taking medications, or memory loss, then a move to an assisted living community may be the next step on the continuum of care. Unless the condition worsens or a terminal illness develops, skilled care in a nursing home will probably never be required. Helping people avoid nursing home care and receive care in a more comfortable setting is a bright spot in the generally somber subject of long-term care.

The myth that a need for long-term care must automatically lead to nursing home confinement exists because at one time, nursing homes were the first, last, and ONLY option available for those who required care but could no longer live at home. Now, nursing homes are just one of many environments in an expanding continuum of long-term care options. In fact, due to the more positive options of home care and assisted living communities, nursing homes are now utilized less often for *true* long-term care—a trend that is expected to continue.

As our population continues to age, it's anticipated that delivery systems currently unknown will become common. Not only will this have the obvious effect of providing the most appropriate level of services, it will also encourage people to become more comfortable with facing the difficult issue of planning ahead for long-term care.

THE VARIOUS LONG-TERM CARE SETTINGS

The Family Home

Most people who need care prefer to remain in familiar surroundings for as long as possible. The preferred environment for receiving long-term care is and always has been the family home, which is where the continuum of care begins. Over 10 million people currently receive care at home, and home care is projected to increase by 178% by 2030.

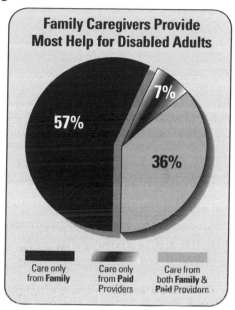

Family Caregivers Provide Most Help for Disabled Adults

57%

7%

36%

Care only from **Family**

Care only from **Paid** Providers

Care from both **Family** & **Paid** Providers

Although the lower cost of home care is an obvious factor in the decision to receive care at home, most who can afford to pay for institutional care will still remain at home for as long as possible.

According to the *National Long-Term Care Survey*, 57% of all people with a disability rely exclusively on unpaid care from family members or other informal caregivers at home. The study found that "Even among people who need assistance with up to five activities of daily living, about 41% relied entirely on unpaid care [at home]."

Medical advances and training have made home care even more practical by allowing home care providers to administer an ever expanding array of services in a person's own home. Home care is a multi-billion dollar industry that exists to support this preferable environment for long-term care services.

When seeking home care services, as with all other long-term care services, the most satisfied people are those who do research, ask the right questions, and shop for quality providers. The Joint Commission on Accreditation of Healthcare Organizations has a helpful list of questions to ask home health care providers. This information is available on the web at **www.jcaho.org** or by phone at 1-630-792-5000.

Services commonly available as a part of home care include:

- **Health Care** — nursing, physical, and other rehabilitative services, help with medications, monitoring, and medical equipment

- **Personal Care** — assistance with personal hygiene, dressing, bathing, exercise, and getting in and out of bed

- **Nutrition** — meal planning, cooking, meal delivery, or meals at outside community sites

- **Homemaking** — housekeeping, shopping, home repair services, and household paperwork

- **Social and Safety** — escort and transportation services, companions, and coordination of provider services

Not surprisingly, the home care benefit of an LTC insurance policy has been cited as one of the most important reasons for choosing LTC insurance as a plan for long-term care. Home care benefits relieve family members from having to perform physical caregiving tasks, allowing them to be more involved in the emotional aspects of care.

When family members are given a choice of whether or not to help with physical care, positive results follow. Studies have shown that even with paid help, friends and family members continue to provide some of the physical aspects of care. A study by the U.S. Department of Health and Human Services shows that family members still performed 40% of the care themselves, even when their loved one received care from paid providers. Two-thirds of informal caregivers continued providing some level of care even with the presence of professional help. This study proves that formal care delivered by professionals does not completely replace the informal care provided by friends and family members.

This research suggests that people with the ability and determination to remain at home *and* the funds to hire supplemental help will get the best of both worlds: professional help plus the caring support of their loved ones. The ability to hire help greatly reduces the stress on family members and allows them to give more of the emotional support that is so often overlooked by a family caregiver who is overwhelmed with the physical tasks of care. "The two systems [formal and informal caregiving at home] work well together to better meet the needs of the entire family," the study concludes.

Adult Day Centers

Staying at home does not necessarily mean staying at home 24 hours a day. Adult day centers provide people with a safe, supportive, supervised place to stay during the day while their informal caregivers are at work or taking a much-needed respite.

There are almost 4,600 adult day centers in the United States. These centers provide care for 260,000 people each day, and this number will increase substantially as the population ages.

Adult day centers allow people to get out and interact socially, making them more likely to attend to their personal care and focus on outside events, rather than focusing on their disabilities. Socializing has been proven to contribute in a positive way to the overall health of the individual. Studies have shown that adult day centers may actually help people stay at home longer.

Most adult day centers provide well balanced meals and a variety of recreational activities. Many centers can accommodate people with relatively severe disabilities. Some even offer preventative health services and therapeutic activities.

The National Adult Day Services Association is a nonprofit association that can help you locate adult day services in your area. Additional information can be found on their website at **www.nadsa.org** or by calling 1-877-745-1440.

Senior Centers

Senior centers are places where "older adults can come together for services and activities that reflect their experience and skills, respond to their diverse needs and interests, enhance their dignity, and support their independence." (National Council on Aging, **www.ncoa.org/content**) Several research studies have found that participation in senior center activities has a positive impact on individual growth and feelings of self-worth. Originally intended solely for social interaction, they are now becoming more comprehensive with a growing emphasis on community service and involvement. As a sign of the times, many are adding new services, such as training in computer skills.

There are now 16,000 senior centers across the country that serve approximately 11 million older adults every year. The services provided by these centers are funded in part by the Older Americans Act, the YMCA, and United Way.

Adult Day Centers

- Nearly **78%** of adult day centers are operated on a nonprofit or public basis.

- **74%** of adult day centers are affiliated with larger organizations, such as home care, skilled nursing facilities, medical centers, or multi-purpose senior organizations.

- The average age of the adult day center participant is 72; two-thirds are women.

- **50%** of those using adult day centers nationwide have some cognitive impairment; one-third require nursing services at least weekly.

- **59%** of those using adult day centers require assistance with two or more activities of daily living. **41%** require assistance with three or more activities of daily living.

National Adult Day Services Association

Multipurpose senior centers are a gateway to the National Aging Services Network, which includes more than 30,000 local, regional, and national service providers for older adults and their caregivers. These centers are often the source of vital community-based social and nutritional support, which allows older Americans to remain independent. Their objective, however, is to serve both active and frail elders.

Typical services include:

- Health and wellness programs
- Meals and nutritional services
- Education in arts and humanities
- Intergenerational programs
- Employment assistance
- Community action and volunteer opportunities
- Transportation
- Leisure travel
- Financial assistance
- Information and referrals

By using a combination of adult day center and senior center services, thousands of people are able to significantly extend the time they can stay in their home environment. But if a person's health declines and the management of day-to-day care becomes more complicated, remaining at home may become difficult and costly. At this point on the continuum of care, some other type of residential care environment may be a more realistic option.

Board and Care Homes

Board and care homes can be a good solution for people who need simple assistance, such as help with meal preparation, medication monitoring, and personal care. This option provides a home-like environment and care provided by familiar faces at a relatively low cost.

Board and care homes are private dwellings where a family or group provides care for a limited number of people with disabilities. The typical number of residents is two to ten. Some converted single-family dwellings are allowed to house only five or six residents.

A board and care home may offer residents the same services as an assisted living community, a skilled nursing home, or in some cases, an Alzheimer's facility. Generally, however, most board and care homes do not offer skilled nursing or medical services and are not the solution for severely disabled people. But they can provide a safe, supportive environment for people who want to actively make choices about daily life and health care while maintaining as much independence as possible.

Some board and care homes serve the needs of those with similar conditions. For example, some specialize in care for people in the middle to late stages of Alzheimer's disease. Others only care for early-stage Alzheimer's patients. Some are only licensed to care for those with a mild mental impairment or to assist those who need relatively minor help (reminders, meal service, laundry, housekeeping help, and driving services).

Since the federal government does not certify board and care homes, the quality of care provided can vary widely. In some areas, the local government enforces only minimal regulations with periodic inspections for compliance. Therefore, it is important to find someone you trust to help you with the decision to place a loved one in a board and care home. Have family members, a lawyer, and a financial professional review contracts before entering into an agreement or paying an entrance fee.

Also, do some research on the home, including:
- Checking for complaints with the state licensing agency
- Asking for and checking references
- Making unscheduled, unannounced visits at different hours

Assisted Living Communities

The most common long-term care delivery system for the first three decades of the twenty-first century will be the assisted living community. Assisted living is the fastest growing type of care setting because it meets the needs of people who cannot make it entirely on their own but do not need or want the skilled nursing care and institutional environment of a nursing home. In contrast to nursing homes, typically viewed as places where "old folks go to die," assisted living communities are a relatively recent and promising phenomenon.

The Assisted Living Federation of America defines an assisted living residence as "a combination of housing, personalized support services, and health care designed to meet the needs—both scheduled and unscheduled—of those who need help with the activities of daily living." The ALFA can provide you with an extensive consumer checklist for choosing an assisted living community. Visit their website at **www.alfa.org**.

A major benefit of the assisted living option is the relief of stress experienced by family members, who often find caring for a loved one at home extremely challenging as the loved one's health declines. Choosing to move into assisted living generally means that, although you need assistance, you still value your independence and want to remain in a home-like environment. Assisted living offers a philosophy of care that emphasizes individuality, privacy, and choice.

A typical resident in assisted living is in their 70s or 80s. Common health problems of residents include Alzheimer's disease, slight memory loss, incontinence, and loss of mobility.

Over 1 million Americans live in the 39,105 assisted living communities throughout the country. The demand for assisted living services resulted in a 71% increase in the number of communities built between 1998 and 2011.

Assisted living communities typically offer the following services:

- Health promotion and exercise programs
- Social and recreational services
- Three meals a day in a common dining area
- Housekeeping services
- Assistance with activities such as eating, bathing, dressing, and toileting
- Transportation
- Access to health and medical services
- 24-hour security and staff
- Emergency call systems in each room
- Medication management

The term "assisted living" covers a variety of settings, which can range from remodeled Victorians to high-rise apartments. The typical assisted living residence has from 25 to 120 units, which may vary in size from single rooms to full-size apartments. Accommodations cover the spectrum from luxurious to spartan, with fees to match.

The cost of care in assisted living communities is less than the cost of nursing home care and, in many cases, can be more economical than home care. For example, assisted living care for a patient with Alzheimer's costs 19% less than the same care provided at home.

Assisted living is paid for with private dollars; residents or their families normally pay the bill out of pocket. One alternative to paying for care with accumulated savings or assets is LTC insurance, which is discussed in detail in later chapters. Although LTC insurance is a relatively new type of insurance, 2.1% of residents in assisted living communities are already paying for care by collecting on their LTC insurance policies.

People in assisted living usually have fewer ADL limitations than those in nursing homes. Nursing home residents use more medical services, skilled nursing care, nutritional services, and social services than assisted living residents. Assisted living residents are much more likely to receive health care services from their private physicians, utilizing transportation services available through the assisted living community.

People in assisted living communities are about twice as likely as nursing home residents to assess their health as "average" or "good." Often, the difference is one of attitude and does not necessarily correlate with the clinical diagnoses or true health of residents. Many people in assisted living simply feel more positive about themselves and their health than those in nursing homes.

Continuing Care Retirement Communities

Continuing Care Retirement Communities (CCRCs) have an awkward name and a high price tag, but they can offer an excellent solution for aging in place for those who can afford the fees. The reasoning behind CCRCs is that people will naturally require higher levels of care and support as they age. Therefore, it makes sense to accommodate the full spectrum of needs on the same campus and within the same community.

CCRCs offer assisted living units, which are usually available in the form of small studio or one-bedroom apartments with scaled-down kitchens. Group dining rooms and common areas for socializing and recreation are often available. A resident may begin their stay in an apartment designed for active, independent living. If their health declines, they may move into assisted living in the same community. If their health continues to decline, they may be able to move into a skilled nursing facility in their community. If the resident recovers or if their health improves, they can easily move back to a lower level of care.

This continuum of care makes a great deal of sense and provides the peace of mind of knowing where you'll be and how you'll receive care, regardless of any changes in your health.

Some of the services typically offered in a CCRC include:
- Nursing and other skilled medical care
- Assisted living
- Personal assistance

Philosophy of Care in Assisted Living

- Offering cost-effective, quality care that is personalized for individual needs
- Fostering independence for each resident
- Treating each resident with dignity and respect
- Promoting the individuality of each resident
- Allowing each resident choice of care and lifestyle
- Protecting each resident's right to privacy
- Nurturing the spirit of each resident
- Involving family and friends
- Providing a safe, residential environment
- Making the assisted living residence a valuable community asset

www.alfa.org/public/articles

- Emergency help
- Meals, including special diet needs
- Housekeeping
- Scheduled transportation
- Recreational, educational, and social activities

If cost were no object, CCRCs, rather than assisted living communities, would be the wave of the future for long-term care delivery. However, cost is very much an issue, and the price of CCRCs is well beyond the means of many people. According to the American Association of Retired Persons (AARP), the up-front entrance fees for CCRCs range from $20,000 to $400,000. Once you pay that lump sum, you still face monthly rent and fees that rival the costs of assisted living communities. But for those with sufficient means, moving into a CCRC can be a permanent solution to a potential need for long-term care, eliminating the stress and uncertainty of how you'll be cared for in the future.

A CCRC resident signs a long-term (normally lifetime) contract when he or she moves on to the campus. The contract is a legal agreement between the resident and the community. You should familiarize yourself with the following three common types of contracts if you are considering this option. The type of contract you agree to will determine the level of service you will receive.

- **Extensive Contracts** — The most expensive option, extensive contracts offer unlimited long-term care for little or no increase in the normal monthly payments.

- **Modified Contracts** — A middle-of-the-road approach, modified contracts provide care for a specified length of time (usually three to five years). Beyond the specified limit, you are responsible for any additional expenses for care.

- **Fee-for-Service** — An agreement that reduces up-front payments but exposes you to potential high costs in the future. Fee-for-service contracts specify that you pay the full rate for all long-term care services you require.

CCRCs sometimes have a group LTC insurance policy that a resident is required to purchase when entering the community. If you are considering moving into a CCRC in the near future, ask the facility administrator about their LTC insurance purchase requirement before you consider purchasing private LTC insurance. Some facilities include LTC insurance as part of their payment fees. If this is the case, you may not need private LTC insurance.

If you already own LTC insurance, ask the facility administrator if the CCRC will waive the requirement to purchase their coverage. If they will not do so, consult your financial advisor prior to canceling your private coverage.

Leading Age provides a consumer directory and additional information about CCRCs on their website at **www.leadingage.org** or by phone at 1-202-783-2242. The Continuing Care Accreditation Commission (CCAC) at **www.carf. org** lists all communities that have met specific standards of certification.

Alzheimer's Facilities

Alzheimer's disease now afflicts approximately 5.4 million Americans and impacts another 14.9 million who have a family member with the disease. By 2025, these figures are projected to grow by 75%.

According to a report published by the U.S. Department of Labor, individuals who suffer from Alzheimer's disease can require care for eight years or longer—the longest average duration of long-term care services. Finding and receiving specialized care can be difficult because people with Alzheimer's disease have a different set of needs than those with simpler age-related health conditions. In addition to assistance with ADLs, they require ongoing social stimulation and close supervision.

Alzheimer's facilities are specifically designed with smaller spaces to accommodate multiple activities. The hallways are designed in a circular fashion, and the residents' doors are often color-coded. Aside from their specialized services and unique design, Alzheimer's facilities are very similar to assisted living communities in most respects.

The Alzheimer's Association (**www.alz.org** or 1-800-272-3900) offers additional information about living options for those with Alzheimer's and support services for their families.

Nursing Homes

Nursing homes are the last stop on the continuum of long-term care. They play a necessary and important role in long-term care, and the continuum of care would not be complete without them.

About 1.6 million people age 65 and older live in nursing homes. The average age of residents is 82, with women constituting the majority of residents.

We place nursing homes last on the continuum of care because:

- Most people will only go into a nursing home as a last resort.
- By planning ahead for long-term care, it is very unlikely you will need to enter a nursing home for an extended period of time.

Nursing homes are by far the most institutional setting on the delivery-of-care spectrum. They are designed to provide mostly medical care to severely physically and cognitively disabled patients during their declining months or years. A variety of studies have shown that elderly patients who spend longer than two years in a nursing facility rarely return home.

Unlike all the other types of care explained earlier, a physician must certify a resident's need for nursing home care. The physician must visit regularly and assume responsibility for the patient's overall treatment of care.

As with any type of long-term care services, the quality of care can vary widely from one nursing home to the next. Unfortunately, the quality of care provided is mostly determined by our ability to pay for care. A nursing home, like any business, must cover its operating costs. This isn't easy with the monies received from Medicaid reimbursements, especially for nursing homes that want to offer high-quality services *(for more on Medicaid see Chapter 4: Who Pays for Long-Term Care?)*. As a result, many nursing homes limit the number of beds available for welfare patients.

Private pay patients are assured "bed availability" and quality care in the facility of their choice. By planning ahead long before there is a need for care, you and your family will have more control over your long-term care delivery options (including possibly avoiding nursing home confinement), as well as the quality of care you receive.

The American Health Care Association is a good resource for information about nursing homes (**www.ahca.org**, 202-842-4444).

Auntie Mae "Blossoms" in Assisted Living

Auntie Mae is the perfect example of the typical assisted living resident. A widow in her 80s, she lived alone for many years, supporting herself by taking on work as a seamstress. During a visit, I noticed she was behaving strangely, almost as if she were having hallucinations. After a visit to the doctor and a subsequent review of her medications, it was determined that Auntie Mae had been taking too much medication. We attempted to organize her medication schedule so she wouldn't forget she had already taken her medication and double-dose. But without someone to remind her, she'd forget to use the reminder system and once again found herself in a drug-induced fog.

At this point, it was clear that Auntie Mae could no longer live by herself. Since she only needed limited assistance and was intent on maintaining her independence—having no desire to move in with her children—assisted living offered the perfect alternative. She now lives in a community that provides her with a personal unit that includes a bedroom, bath, small living room, and kitchenette. She hasn't had any further incidents involving overmedicating because the staff members monitor her schedule. In addition, we've found that the social activities available to her have made her "blossom" and enjoy life again. Both her physical and mental health have improved significantly in this new living arrangement.

— *Kathleen Deknis*

KEY POINTS

Where Is Long-Term Care Received?

➤ *Skilled care* is provided when intensive medical attention is required. Medicare and most private insurance plans cover skilled care.

➤ *Non-skilled care,* also known as *custodial care,* is provided when the prognosis is progressive deterioration over a long period of time (100 days or longer) with little chance of recovery. Custodial care is not covered by Medicare, Medicare Supplement insurance, or private health insurance.

The Continuum of Long-Term Care includes all the settings in which long-term care services are provided:

➤ The **family home** remains the preferred environment for receiving long-term care.

➤ **Board and care homes** are private dwellings that offer care in a home-like environment for a limited number of people who need minor assistance.

➤ **Assisted living communities** provide personal assistance and low-level nursing care, all on the same campus.

➤ **Continuing Care Retirement Communities** offer facilities ranging from apartments for independent and active residents to assisted living arrangements and, in some cases, skilled nursing care.

➤ **Alzheimer's facilities** offer unique floorplans and provide the special care required by those who have been diagnosed with Alzheimer's disease.

➤ **Nursing homes** provide mostly medical care to severely physically and cognitively disabled patients during their declining months or years.

Chapter 3

How Much Does Long-Term Care Cost?

*The future, according to some scientists,
will be exactly like the past, only far more expensive.*

— John Sladde, *Science fiction writer (1937-2000)*

Senator John Heinz was one of the first to understand the importance of having a plan for long-term care. He understood that if you made a list of potential "big ticket items," you probably wouldn't think to include long-term care. Yet long-term care expenses may cost more during your lifetime than any other single expenditure.

Specific costs of long-term care services vary widely. **The three major factors that drive the cost of long-term care are:**

1. **Geographic location:** As with all living expenses, the cost will largely depend on the part of the country where the care is received.

2. **The place in which the care is received:** See *Chapter 2* for an explanation of various environments where care is received, the available levels of care, and the continuum of long-term care services.

> The greatest threat to the financial security of Americans is the cost of long-term care. (We) can insure our cars against theft or damage, our houses against flood, fire, and earthquakes, our children against the costs of college and braces, and our families against the risks of an early death. But when it comes to insuring the single greatest threat to our life savings and emotional reserves—the cost of long-term care—most Americans have no (plan). In many ways, it's as if we're wearing bulletproof vests with holes over our hearts.
>
> *(paraphrased)*
> The late Senator John Heinz,
> Select Committee on Aging

3. **Reason(s) for care:** The severity of the condition causing the need for care can vary the cost by thousands of dollars per month.

The statistics and costs given in this chapter represent national averages for care received in various settings. The specific costs of care in your area can be obtained online at **www.smartltcplan.com.**

GEOGRAPHIC LOCATION AND ENVIRONMENT
Home Care

The national average rate for a nurse to come to your home is $45 per hour. The average rate for a non-skilled caregiver to come to your home is $24 per hour.

FAST FACTS:

- Depending on the severity of the need for care, home care can be the most expensive or the least expensive option.

- **68%** of people 60 and older will receive help from family members and other informal caregivers at some point during their lifetime.

- Women account for **75%** of caregivers 50 and older.

- Among caregivers aged 50–64, **60%** must juggle full or part-time work *and* caregiving.

- **58%** of caregivers must make changes in their work schedules to provide care.

In more expensive areas of the country, however, a visit from a Licensed Practical Nurse can cost over $100 per hour. Even unskilled services can cost more than $35 per hour.

Home care also involves services beyond personnel. When you add up all the average expenses for home care—including personnel, medical equipment, and supplies—the average total cost for daily home care is $97.

Assisted Living Communities

Assisted living communities will provide most long-term care services for at least the next two decades. They offer a more pleasant and positive living environment than nursing homes at a lower cost.

Most assisted living communities charge by the month. The average national cost of care per month is $3,477, but the costs can vary from a low of $2,150 per month to a high of $6,500 per month or more.

These figures do not include care beyond assistance with two activities of daily living. People who need care above and beyond this basic level will incur additional costs. Still, compared to nursing home care and, in some instances, home care, assisted living communities offer one of the best values in long-term care delivery.

Nursing Homes

The national average daily rate for nursing home care is $226 for a private room and $206 for a semi-private room. That comes to an average *annual* cost of over $82,000 for a private room and over $75,000 for semi-private accommodations.

But the actual cost of care in a nursing home varies almost as widely as home care and is mainly influenced by city and region. For example, in Orlando, a private room is a relative bargain at $204 per day, compared to high cost cities such as Boston at $306 per day and San Francisco at $307 per day.

However, these figures may be misleading and actually lower than the true cost of care in a nursing home. Medicaid, the welfare program, pays for nursing home care for those who are impoverished. Analysts point out that most nursing homes lose money on Medicaid patients because they must accept Medicaid's low reimbursement rates. This results in Medicaid services being delivered at less than true market value. These low reimbursement payments are included in the averaging of nursing home costs and thus may distort the true average cost of nursing home care. (See *Chapter 4* for a more detailed explanation of Medicaid)

REASONS FOR CARE

In addition to your geographic location and the environment in which long-term care is received, the reasons for long-term care have a major impact on its cost. Some long-term care services, such as minor assistance with ADLs, can be relatively inexpensive. Specialized types of care, such as services provided to people with Alzheimer's disease, are expensive by comparison. In fact, the average amount spent over a lifetime on long-term care for an Alzheimer's patient is $320,000, making it the third most expensive condition in the United States behind heart disease and cancer.

THE IMPORTANCE OF CONSIDERING INFLATION

In developing a plan for long-term care, the most relevant figures are not the costs of care today but the projected costs taking into consideration the effects of inflation. Once you have developed your plan, it is wise to review it every year and make sure it takes into consideration the newly inflated costs of care.

The rate of inflation for long-term care expenses has remained at a reasonable level in recent years, a trend that is predicted to continue due to the surge in availability of reasonably priced assisted living communities. Specifically, expenses are predicted to rise at an annual rate of between 4% and 7% between now and 2018.

But the demand for long-term care services—due to baby boomers moving into their 70s and 80s—could result in long-term care inflation rates approaching double digits after 2018. It is imperative that you monitor the actual inflation rates in future years so your plan for long-term care accomplishes its objectives.

THE SILENT COSTS OF LONG-TERM CARE

The costs of care from a line-item standpoint do not tell the entire story. The physical, emotional, and psychological impact on caregivers, as well as lost income opportunities,

IMPACT OF FAMILY CAREGIVING ON CAREERS

40%	Unable to advance in careers
75%	Affects their health
66%	Affects their lifetime earnings
96%	Make informal workplace adjustments
84%	Make formal workplace adjustments

Family Caregivers: Physical & Emotional Burdens

In considering the role of caregiver, it's important to measure the physical and emotional exhaustion that might be experienced by a caregiver trying to care for a full-sized adult—in some cases one twice the size of the caregiver. Answer these questions truthfully to determine if you would realistically be able to take on the role of caregiver:

- Will I be able to help him/her transfer in and out of bed? On and off the toilet?

- Will I be able to roll him/her over in bed to change clothing and bedding?

- Will I be able to help him/her bathe or shower?

- Will I be able to get him/her dressed and undressed?

- Will I feel comfortable providing personal care and hygiene for him/her?

must also be included in any discussion about the true costs of long-term care.

Family Care: The Loss in Income and Assets

Most caregivers are family members who attempt to maintain their careers while caring for a loved one. Over half of those providing care are employed full-time, while another 13% work part time.

We usually think of family caregivers as providing care "free of charge," but the fact is that those who balance caregiving and employment pay a heavy price for their caregiving responsibilities. Although most family caregivers begin by simply providing occasional assistance to a relative or spouse, many of those providing care eventually alter their lifestyle and career choices.

A series of surveys called "The Juggling Act Study" attempted to measure the financial consequences of balancing caregiving with work. A large majority of family caregivers reported the need for flexible hours—arriving at work late or leaving early—and for taking time off during the day. They also had to use sick leave and vacation time to fulfill their caregiving obligations. Family caregivers reported other common strategies to juggle career and caregiving, including cutting down on work hours, taking a leave of absence, switching to part-time work, quitting their job entirely, or retiring early.

By measuring the "cumulative effects from wage reductions, lost retirement and pension benefits, compromised opportunities for training/promotion, and stress-related health problems," the study found that family caregivers sacrifice an astonishing amount of earning potential. "The average total financial loss as a result of caregiving by a family member is estimated at $659,139 over the lifetime (of the caregiver)."

The Average Length of Family Caregiving

Most family members who provide care never anticipated becoming care-givers. For those who did consider becoming caregivers, few accurately estimated the number of hours per week they would eventually devote to caregiving or the ultimate duration of the care. The majority of participants in the survey estimated they would need to provide care from six months to two years. The actual average length of family caregiving is eight years!

Given the stress and time pressures they faced, it comes as no surprise that three quarters of participants reported that caregiving had adversely affected their own health. More than 20% experienced a significant decline in health and an increase in the number of visits to their own health care providers.

The Sandwich Generation: Time, Energy, and Money Spread Thin Between Elderly and Children

A growing challenge for many families is the emergence of the "sandwich generation": people who are caught in the middle of caring for an older relative while still raising their children.

The financial, physical, and emotional burdens of providing care while rais-ing children have a severely negative impact on these families. The time and attention once given to children and spouses are diverted to an ailing parent. The caregiver's physical energy is depleted as they strive to juggle their care-giving duties with maintaining a healthy family life. The time and money they once accrued for family vacations is now used to supplement the care and services needed by the ill family member.

The costs associated with caregiving are not simply measured in dollars. All too often, the costs are evident in a strained relationship with a spouse, behav-ioral problems in a child, or the emotional and/or physical breakdown of the caregiver as a result of spreading herself too thin. These are the "silent" costs of long-term care—costs *in addition* to the direct financial costs.

BREAKING THE ICE WITH YOUR PARENTS

Warm Ways to Get the Conversation Started About Creating a Smart LTC Plan

Fortunately, grown children and their parents are finally beginning to feel comfortable having the "long-term care conversation". How you enter this terrain will depend on the relationship you have with your parents.

You may not get far in your first conversation. It's a lot to digest, particularly if your parents have avoided this subject. Be patient. Find what works for you. If one approach doesn't work, try another.

To get started, here are a few ways to break the ice:

- **Be Open** – If you have an open and direct relationship, don't beat around the bush. Just come out and tell them that you'd like to talk about these issues.

- **Be Reflective** – Some time when you're together, ask them about their past, their childhood, and their parents. Learn more about them. Then move on to the future. What do they want most? How do they perceive the future? What worries them?

- **Discuss Someone Else's Situation** – This is often the easiest and most logical approach. Chances are that you or your parents know someone who is already dealing with some aspect of aging or long-term care. Talking about what's good or bad about their situation can be a useful launching point.

- **Ask for Advice** – This is a great way to get the discussion rolling. Tell them that you just met with a financial advisor and that you're preparing for the future. Then ask them for advice. Follow that by asking how they've planned ahead.

- **Grab an Opening** – If, for example, your mother is talking about Aunt Kathy, who's in an assisted living facility, and rolls her eyes and says, "Don't you ever put me in one of those places," ask her what she means. What would your mother want in the same circumstance? If you miss the chance, bring it up another time. "Hey Mom, remember when we talked about Aunt Kathy and you said "Don't you ever put me in one of those places"? . . . .

- **Write** – If you find the whole thing too daunting, write a letter or e-mail outlining your concerns and what you would like to discuss. This can be particularly helpful if you live far away and only have a weekend to have these talks. You can pave the way and get them to start thinking about it before you get together.

- **Get Help** – Maybe you have a sibling who is more at ease talking with your parents. Maybe your parents are more comfortable talking to someone else in the family about finances or health. Don't be offended. You don't care how the plan gets developed, just that it **DOES** get developed.

- **Suggest** – That they peruse or read this book. They can also get help at **www.smartltcplan.com.**

- **Recommend** – That they seek advice from an *Objective Financial Advisor* on how to plan ahead. (More details about these advisors are explained in *Chapter 6*)

Grandmother Changed "Overnight"

My husband's grandmother was always meticulous about her housekeeping and was an impeccable dresser. We were naturally shocked when my husband went to take her to lunch one day and found her still in her robe and looking confused, her house in disarray. He knew something was terribly wrong and immediately called his mother. An appointment was arranged for the grandmother to be evaluated by her doctor. Her doctor's assessment, followed by subsequent testing, confirmed that she was in the early stages of dementia.

The family decided it was no longer safe for her to live alone and moved her into an assisted living community close by. The cost of care at that time was $2,000 per month. After several years, she was diagnosed with Alzheimer's and required more care than the assisted living community could provide. She was eventually moved into a nursing home. She passed away 14 years later. While settling her affairs, we made the last monthly payment to the nursing home: **$12,000!**

— Ruth Simpson

KEY POINTS

How Much Does Long-Term Care Cost?

➤ The factors that determine the costs of long-term care are geographic location, environment where care is received, and the severity of the person's condition.

➤ Assisted living communities charge by the month and costs can vary from a low of $2,150/month to a high of $6,500/month or more.

➤ The average annual cost of a nursing home care is over $82,000 for a private room and over $75,000 for a semi-private room.

➤ The predicted average annual rate of inflation for the cost of long-term care in the next few years is between 4% and 7%. Beyond 2018, double-digit inflation is likely due to the need for long-term care by aging baby boomers.

➤ The average total financial loss as a result of caregiving by a family member is estimated to be $659,139 over the caregiver's lifetime.

➤ The silent costs of caregiving by family members include an impact on current lifestyle and career goals, postponement of retirement, stress-related health problems, and strained personal relationships.

➤ The phrase "sandwich generation" is often used to define people caught in the middle of caring for an older relative while still raising children.

Chapter 4   Who Pays for Long-Term Care?

We have not passed that subtle line
between childhood and adulthood until...
we have stopped saying "It got lost"
and start saying "I lost it."

— Sidney J. Harris

Sources of funding for long-term care expenses are a major concern for our state and federal governments because long-term care expenditures could expand to the point of dwarfing our current "health care crisis." An increase in life expectancy, the size of the baby boom generation, and the inflation of health care costs are driving this expensive problem.

With the help of financial advisors, government analysts, and experts on aging, Americans are beginning to understand that long-term care expenses could be the greatest risk to their financial security. Due to new awareness of this financial and emotional risk, many Americans are taking action by pre-planning (as opposed to crisis planning) to protect their families and their legacies against the impact of long-term care.

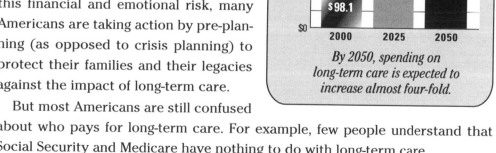

Growth in Long-Term Care Spending

By 2050, spending on long-term care is expected to increase almost four-fold.

But most Americans are still confused about who pays for long-term care. For example, few people understand that Social Security and Medicare have nothing to do with long-term care.

There are four sources for providing or paying for long-term care:

1. Family

2. Medicaid (Medi-Cal in California), the welfare program

3. Personal assets

4. Long-term care insurance

FAST FACTS:
WHAT WE DON'T KNOW CAN HURT US

- **71%** of Medicare recipients mistakenly believe Medicare is a primary source for covering long-term care.

- Most people mistakenly believe a Medicare Supplement policy will pay for long-term care.

- **87%** of people under age 65 mistakenly believe their private health insurance will cover the cost of long-term care.

Some of the pros and cons of these sources are explained below. Long-term care insurance is explained only briefly because an in-depth discussion of insurance is provided in future chapters.

At the end of this chapter, we dispel some myths about other sources commonly believed to cover long-term care and provide you with a clearer understanding of what these programs actually do and don't cover.

FAMILY

When a loved one needed care in past decades, other family members took on the role of caregiver. Women—usually wives, daughters, or daughters-in-law—were the most likely care providers for immediate and extended family members.

But changes have occurred in our society that make it less likely that our family will be in a position to provide our care. Families today are not only much smaller, but many are also spread across the globe, with two careers required to support the family's financial obligations. Even relying on a spouse for care may not be an option due to changes in the traditional American family structure. In the future, *paid* caregivers will be the most common providers of long-term care services.

As explained in *Chapter 3,* caring for a loved one is a necessity for many families who failed to deliberately plan for long-term care. According to a study conducted by the National Alliance for Caregivers, the number of U.S. households providing care to adults aged 50 and older has more than quadrupled in the past 13 years. According to AARP, 22.4 million adult children are providing care for their elderly parents. The average caregiver is a married, middle-class woman in her late 40s caring for her mother-in-law and/or her own mother, usually in that order. 28% of caregivers are men. Over half of those providing care are employed full time and another 13% work part time. According to another report released in 2007, these caregivers experience the highest rates of depression among all U.S. workers.

Some well-meaning children insist they will personally provide for their parents' long-term care. This is contrary to the wishes of most parents, who will do almost anything to keep from becoming a burden on their children.

But if you decide that relying on your family *is* a viable option for your plan for care, talk seriously with your spouse and children about the type of care they can and will provide. This option should be put in writing by completing your online assessment at **www.smartltcplan.com.** This will ensure that everyone's responsibilities are clearly outlined in writing. It may also be a good idea to have your family members present when developing the specifics of your plan because the need for care often has less impact on the person in need of care than it has on the rest of the family.

MEDICAID, THE WELFARE PROGRAM

Medicaid provides funding for approximately 45% of all long-term care expenses in the United States. The federal and state-funded program began in 1965 to provide medical care for impoverished, elderly, blind, and disabled persons who could not afford the cost of care. The lack of other payment options, especially for nursing home care, has resulted in a large portion of nursing home residents relying solely on the Medicaid program to pay for their care.

Eligibility for Medicaid

Medicaid laws have been revised many times since the creation of the program, which has resulted in a convoluted legal structure used to determine eligibility for Medicaid benefits. There are various "look-back periods" if you transfer assets, as well as asset transfer penalties, income caps, and waiting periods.

Medicaid is a needs-based program whereby eligibility is determined by an evaluation of a person's assets and income. The rules are complex, vary between states, and are subject to change every year. Although the federal government issues guidelines regarding benefits, each state is allowed to implement these guidelines according to their own interpretation of them. The Medicaid program varies so widely in the amount and duration of benefits, the United States has experienced a growing phenomenon called "Medicaid Migration": the act of moving from state to state in search of the most generous benefits. At present, the phenomenon is small, but it demonstrates the seriousness of the long-term care dilemma.

Eligibility for Medicaid generally requires that an applicant meet five requirements:

1. *Citizenship.* A Medicaid long-term care beneficiary must be a U.S. citizen or a "qualified alien" (for example, a permanent resident, refugee, asylee, or person granted conditional entry).

2. *Residence.* The applicant must be a resident of the state where the application is filed.

3. *Medical Need.* In order to qualify for long term-care assistance, the applicant must demonstrate a need for long-term care. Each state has its own method of determining if this need exists. Typically, the applicant must show impairment with several "activities of daily living," such as eating, dressing, and bathing.

4. *Resources.* The applicant may not have more than the allowable amount of assets. But an asset is not simply an asset; it must be classified as exempt, non-exempt, available, or unavailable. What is considered exempt or unavailable varies from state to state, but typically a single applicant may have no more than $2,000 in available assets in addition to exempt assets such as their residence. There are special rules and exceptions for married couples to guard against "spousal impoverishment." These rules and exceptions also vary from state to state.

5. *Income.* In "medically needy" states, income eligibility is met by having an income too low to cover the actual cost of care. However, nearly half of the states employ an "income cap" to determine whether an applicant qualifies for Medicaid. Individuals who meet the other requirements but whose incomes exceed the cap will not be eligible.

Share of Cost

In "medically needy" states, where excess income does not trigger ineligibility, the state sets a "maintenance need standard," or an amount of the beneficiary's income that may be allocated to living expenses. Individuals whose monthly incomes are higher than this set limit must pay for their care with the difference between their income and the set maintenance need standard. Known as the "share of cost," this money is essentially a copayment for medical and nursing home costs. The beneficiary is responsible for this share of cost before Medicaid will cover the remaining balance of the state's agreed-upon cost of care each month. The amount a nursing home resident is allowed to retain after paying their share of cost is as low as $35 per month in some states.

Accessibility of Care

Medicaid licensed providers are reimbursed by the government, but the payment is less than the private pay rate. As a result, nursing homes that have a high number of Medicaid patients generate less income than non-Medicaid nursing homes. For this reason, a private pay patient will generally be given priority admission over a Medicaid patient. Medicaid recipients are sometimes placed on a waiting list to enter a facility even if there are beds available. In the meantime, they must rely on other resources for care—resources that may be inadequate, further compromising their health. This practice is common because only a few states have enacted laws prohibiting admission practices based on the source of payment.

For most people in need of long-term care, receiving care at home or in an assisted living environment is emotionally preferable to moving into a nursing home. But in general, high quality care at home or in assisted living is reserved for private pay patients.

Quality of Care Issues

There is an ongoing debate regarding the difference between the quality of care received by Medicaid beneficiaries and care received by private pay patients. For example, my wife's grandmother paid for her long-term care services with her own money until she became impoverished and was forced to rely on welfare. The quality of care she received while she was "private pay" was noticeably superior to the care she received once she was on welfare. *(See "When the Money Under the Mattress Is Gone" at the end of this chapter.)*

Evidence that there may be a quality of care deficency for Medicaid patients was brought to light in November 2001 by the ERISA (Employee Retirement Income Security Act) Advisory Council with the statement, "Medicaid reimbursement rates are so low that they may compromise quality of care, as well as the financial viability of the long-term care industry."

Medicaid Planning

Medicaid Planning is the process of positioning your income and assets so you can legally qualify for Medicaid. Despite stories of "millionaires on Medicaid," the vast majority of people who enlist professional assistance with Medicaid Planning are not wealthy. Because of quality of care deficiencies with Medicaid, it would be foolish for individuals who can afford private pay care to divest themselves of their assets to receive government-paid care.

Medicaid Planning may be the only option for some people. For example, some people have health conditions that will make it impossible to qualify for long-term care insurance. Someone in this situation must consider using one of the remaining resources for paying for care.

The process of Medicaid Planning has a bad reputation because some unscrupulous practitioners have abused the system and taken unfair advantage of taxpayers. This problem arises because there is no uniform regulation for companies or individuals who call themselves Medicaid Planners. Beware of practitioners who offer Medicaid Planning with the true motive of exposing your assets to sell you financial products that may or may not be appropriate for your situation. The most ethical professionals are licensed attorneys who are regulated by their state bar associations and

utilize a process that professionally guides you through the myriad of complicated Medicaid rules. When considering Medicaid Planning, be sure to consult
with a licensed attorney who is experienced in this area.

Estate Recovery

Estate Recovery is a program that reimburses the government for money
spent by Medicaid for a beneficiary's care. This money is recovered from a
deceased Medicaid beneficiary's estate. States' efforts to recapture this money
are becoming more aggressive, closing any loopholes that allow Medicaid beneficiaries to leave money to family members until the government is reimbursed.
Estate Recovery is now a required program in every state.

The Future of Medicaid

The Medicaid program is a lifesaver for some in need of care, but the
ongoing expansion of the program has strained our government's budget. The
availability of government funding for long-term care through Medicaid is likely
to decrease sharply in the decades ahead. For baby boomers and their children,
planning ahead for a time when Medicaid will not be readily available is the
wisest decision they can make for securing high quality and affordable care.

PERSONAL ASSETS

Americans spend billions of dollars in personal assets annually on long-term
care expenses. The dollar value of personal assets used to pay for care is predicted to double between 2010 and 2015. Personal assets used to pay for care
are normally withdrawn from one or more of three places: personal savings,
retirement accounts, and home equity.

When considering this option, analyze:

- Your ability to accumulate enough assets to pay for long-term care
  expenses

- The impact on your family of risking your assets. Even if you can accumulate the necessary funds to pay for your care, a long-term care event will
  likely affect your family's standard of living.

- Your legacy, and whether or not you wish to leave assets to heirs.

If you *do* choose to rely on your personal assets, having a written plan for
long-term care will spare you and your family of any unpleasant surprises.
Make sure the plan deliberately identifies and earmarks the funds you wish to
be used to pay for your care.

LONG-TERM CARE INSURANCE

Long-term care insurance is specifically designed to cover long-term care expenses. Insurance can pay for care in a nursing home, assisted living community, at home, or in an adult day center.

Only about 4% of the population owns coverage because this type of insurance has only been available for two decades. But as Americans become more knowledgeable about the need to plan ahead, LTC insurance is expected to become a major payer of long-term care expenses. By 2025, it's predicted that LTC insurance will pay a larger share of long-term care expenses than any other source, other than welfare.

We devote several chapters of this book to a complete discussion of LTC insurance as an option for paying for long-term care.

MYTH: OTHER RESOURCES WILL PAY FOR LONG-TERM CARE

Most families are as shocked as we were when we learned that Medicare and Medicare Supplement policies would not pay for my grandfather's long-term care expenses. Private health insurance plans also specifically *exclude* coverage for long-term care.

WHO PAYS FOR WHAT TYPES OF CARE?

	Reliance on Family	Welfare	Personal Assets	LTC Insurance
Home Care	?	Limited	Yes	Yes
Community Based Services	?	No	Yes	Yes
Adult Day Center	?	No	Yes	Yes
Assisted Living	?	No	Yes	Yes
Continuing Care Retirement Communities	?	No for Independent and Assisted Living; Limited for other care	Yes	No for Independent Living; Yes for all other care
Hospital Care	?	Yes	Yes	No
Skilled Nursing Home	?	Yes	Yes	Yes
Non-Skilled Nursing Home	?	Yes	Yes	Yes

Medicare

Medicare provides health insurance coverage to Americans over 65 and to some people with disabilities who are under 65. Studies have shown that 71% of Medicare recipients believe Medicare is a primary source for paying for long-term care. But Medicare was enacted as a benefit to pay for physician and hospital care and does not cover the expenses associated with the care of people who simply need assistance with activities of daily living or supervision due to cognitive impairment.

The myth about Medicare covering long-term care is due to the wording in the *Medicare Handbook (U.S. Health and Human Services, 2012)*. The handbook explains that, under certain conditions, Medicare covers the first 20 days in a skilled nursing home and another 80 days of care on a co-payment basis. But care with a duration of less than 100 days is *short-term care*.

Medicare's "short-term care" benefit is designed to partially cover rehabilitation from a serious injury or illness. A three-day prior hospitalization is required to qualify for benefits, and care must be provided in an approved *skilled* nursing home. Custodial care, the most common level of care, is not covered by Medicare.

Private Benefits

■ **Medicare Supplement Insurance**

Medicare Supplement policies only cover services *approved* by Medicare. These policies do not cover long-term care.

Medicare Supplement policies may supplement short-term care. Specifically, Medicare Supplement coverage may offer a co-payment benefit for care given by approved providers, beginning on the 21st day of care and continuing for up to 100 days in an approved *skilled* nursing home. This skilled care must also be preceded by a three-day hospitalization.

■ **Health Insurance**

Health insurance, like Medicare, is only a provider of "short-term care." Health care benefits cover most Americans against illness and accidents but specifically exclude long-term care coverage. The maximum benefit for care provided by health insurance plans is 100 days.

When the Money
Under the Mattress Is Gone

Having lived through the Great Depression of the 1930s, Nana and Gramps lived very frugally on my grandfather's salary as a construction worker. As a result of careful planning, after Gramps passed away, my grandmother was able to live comfortably on the money they had stashed away under the mattress (literally!).

When Nana first went into a nursing home, she went in as a "private pay" patient. Allen and I were very impressed with the facility the first few times we went to visit her.

Within a few months, Nana had spent all of her savings and was officially a Medicaid (welfare) patient. No longer on the first floor, Nana was "housed" on the second floor—away from the beautiful lobby with fresh flowers, the library with original works of art, and the community room where social activities took place. Our first impression of a caring facility was suddenly replaced by genuine concern for her well-being as we noticed a "distinct odor" permeating the hallway. Not long after that, Nana became bedridden and—within a few weeks of going on Medicaid—passed away.

Would Nana have deteriorated so fast if she had remained a private pay patient? We'll never know the answer to that question.

— *Eileen Hamm*

KEY POINTS

Who Pays for Long-Term Care?

➤ There are four sources for providing or paying for long-term care: family, welfare, personal assets, and long-term care insurance.

➤ Welfare coverage is only available after a person's assets have been depleted.

➤ Waiting lists for "Medicaid only" beds exist because few states have enacted laws that prohibit admission policies based on source of payment.

➤ When considering Medicaid Planning, be sure to consult with a licensed attorney who is experienced in this area.

➤ Heirs are often surprised to learn they are required to reimburse a portion of their inheritance to repay the government for long-term care provided to their loved ones through the Medicaid program. This process is called "Estate Recovery."

➤ Long-term care insurance is specifically designed to cover long-term care expenses in an adult day center, at home, in an assisted living community, or in a nursing home.

➤ Medicare does not pay for long-term care. The program was established to pay for physician and hospital care and does not cover costs associated with the care of people who simply need assistance with activities of daily living or supervision due to cognitive impairment.

➤ Medicare Supplement policies only cover services approved by Medicare and do not cover long-term care.

➤ Private health insurance specifically excludes coverage for long-term care. The maximum amount of benefit for care provided by health insurance is 100 days.

Chapter 5 **Why Is Long-Term Care a Women's Issue?**
by Eileen Hamm

As a woman and a registered nurse, I know that the person who provides the care is generally the female. "We" usually means "she," especially when it comes to taking care of a spouse, parents of a spouse, or one's own parents.

— Eileen Hamm

Having a written plan for long-term care is important for every family in America, but this is particularly true for women. Almost always, the female takes ultimate responsibility for the day-to-day care of a family member who is ill or disabled. This is not sexist. This is not whining. It's a fact. In our years of working with financial professionals to assist families with LTC Planning, I have personally listened to the stories of women whose lives have been completely altered due to the long-term care needs of a loved one. Similar stories involving men are also becoming more common, but the majority of informal caregivers in our country—almost 72% of the estimated 7 million providers of care—are female.

When I talk with couples about planning for long-term care, they often exchange glances and say, "Oh, we'll take care of one another when the time comes." This pledge of mutual aid between spouses is touching and undoubtedly sincere, but it usually comes from those who have yet to observe someone in their personal circle move from independence to a need for sustained care. Those who have closely observed others struggling with a long-term care need are typically driven to develop a realistic plan for long-term care, and that plan rarely includes the option of deliberately relying on family.

My paternal grandmother, Nana, is a good example of how long-term care affects women. After my grandfather passed away, my father made sure Nana was safe and received the attention she needed. During the many years she was healthy, he took the place of his father by being "on call" to help her with day-to-day living. He accompanied her to doctor visits, took her shopping, and called her every day. But when Nana's health declined and she needed assistance with personal care, my father's involvement lessened and my mother took over the major responsibilities of Nana's care. It was my mother, Nana's daughter-in-law, who handled the intimate tasks of helping her in and out of bed, bathing her, and dressing her. This is a very typical pattern: As the level of care required grows more personal and intimate, the male caregivers in the family begin to feel uncomfortable, and the women take over the primary role of caregiver. Women tend to be more comfortable and skilled in this role, especially if they've also had children. But providing care comes with a heavy price; with the accompanying emotional and physical stress of being a caregiver, a woman has a 63% higher risk of dying earlier than a woman of the same age who does not become a caregiver.

Women often sacrifice their social network and sense of well-being to care for a loved one. It seems that every time I talk with my mother, who is now in her 80s, she tells me about a sister or a friend "having an awful time" taking care of a spouse. These women tell her about the pure physical exhaustion they experience from caring for an adult on a daily basis. They suffer from the depression that comes from shouldering the responsibility alone, and they feel guilty for not being able to "do more."

But the prospect of becoming a caregiver is not the only reason women should ask their financial professional about LTC Planning for their family—it's also vital that they plan for *their own* care. Women make up the largest percentage of residents in all types of long-term care facilities, with the majority being widowed or divorced. Because we usually marry men at least a few years older than ourselves, and we live about seven years longer than men, only 13% of women are still married by age 85.

By contrast, men make up the majority of people being taken care of at home. A wife or daughter usually helps her husband and parents through to the end, but then her resources are limited when *she* needs long-term care. Unable to rely on informal, unpaid care from relatives at home, women are usually forced to rely on more formal and costly solutions, such as entering a nursing home.

For example, although both my grandfathers lived to a ripe old age, neither of them spent time in a nursing home or any other type of care facility. As both grandfathers became weaker and more debilitated due to old age and illness, my grandmothers once again found themselves in a mothering role, this time responsible for their husbands' daily care at home. By contrast, both my grandmothers spent their last years in care facilities, progressing from senior apartments to assisted living communities, and finally to nursing homes. This is the typical trend: A husband can generally count on receiving good care provided by his spouse in his own home. If his wife can't provide the care personally, she will use their assets to hire and supervise full or part-time caregivers.

Could I be a caregiver for my husband? Sure I could. Do I want to? No. Does this mean I care less for my spouse? That I'm a selfish person? No. It means I care enough to plan and make sure my family and I have choices if someone we love requires long-term care.

Choices for women were limited in earlier generations. Thankfully, we now have access to the knowledge and resources required to actively participate in planning ahead for our family's well-being. We will always be "caretakers," but our role today includes careful advanced planning for the potential long-term care of our loved ones *and ourselves.* If we don't proactively plan ahead, the comfortable and financially secure retirement we envision could be greatly altered or even cut short by the consequences of providing or receiving long-term care.

KEY POINTS

Why Is Long-Term Care a Women's Issue?

➤ The majority of informal caregivers in our country—almost 72% of the estimated 7 million providers of care—are female.

➤ Women make up the largest percentage of residents in all types of long-term care facilities.

➤ Men make up the largest percentage of people receiving care at home because a spouse, daughter, or daughter-in-law normally provides care for as long as possible.

➤ A female caregiver has a 63% higher risk of dying earlier than a woman of the same age who does not become a caregiver.

PART 2

The Only Effective Way to Plan for Long-Term Care

Lack of planning on your part does not constitute an emergency on my part.

— Anonymous

PART 2:
The Only Effective Way to
Plan for Long-Term Care

Long-term care planning is heavily influenced by the insurance industry because LTC insurance was invented and extensively promoted prior to the need for most Americans to have a plan for long-term care. It was initially created as an additional type of insurance for traditional insurance agents to sell but was deemed worthless by reputable financial professionals. Over the years, with the aid of legislation, insurance to pay for long-term care became a viable option for some families.

Although LTC insurance is not for everyone, the need to have a plan for long-term care is essential. But the continued perception that the two terms, LTC Planning and LTC insurance, are synonymous is why millions of Americans fail to plan ahead for long-term care. Traditional insurance agents promote insurance using such phrases as, "LTC insurance is for everyone" and "LTC insurance should be as common as car insurance." These types of statements, along with the aggressive sales approaches used by these agents naturally cause most Americans to be suspicious and to ignore LTC Planning in general.

The *Smart LTC Planning*™ process (explained in *Chapter 7*) solves this problem. It evaluates all of your options for paying for long-term care, not just LTC insurance, from the perspective of your unique situation. You can access online tools that help you with this process by going to **www.smartltcplan.com.**

The *Smart LTC Planning*™ process views LTC Planning as an integral component of financial and estate planning. Embracing this viewpoint makes it apparent that the person to initiate your LTC Plan is not an insurance agent, but a financial advisor. We specifically recommend utilizing the services of an *Objective Financial Advisor*. These advisors have a specific set of skills and competencies, which are explained in *Chapter 6*. Page 63 explains how to find one.

Chapter **6** Utilizing the Services of an *Objective Financial Advisor*

In theory, theory and practice are the same.
In practice they're not.

— Yogi Berra

Throughout this book, I've recommended that you plan for long-term care within the context of your total financial picture. I've made it clear that insurance agents should be avoided when it comes to planning ahead because their only goal may be to sell you LTC insurance. While insurance may be an appropriate option, you can't know that until you objectively evaluate it, along with your other options, within the context of your personal situation. You should seek the services of an *Objective Financial Advisor* to assist you with LTC Planning. But first, read this book and then complete the online assessment at **www.smartltcplan.com.**

THE DIFFERENCES BETWEEN *OBJECTIVE FINANCIAL ADVISORS* AND OTHER FINANCIAL ADVISORS

Most people are confused when it comes to who they should trust with their financial future. Intuitively, most of us know that all financial advisors are *not* created equal.

The most important differences between an *Objective Financial Advisor* and a traditional financial advisor have to do with their:

- Philosophy concerning their relationship with you
- Approach toward providing the services they offer
- Compensation
- Willingness to assist with "psychology of money" issues

RELATIONSHIPS VS. TRANSACTIONS

Objective Financial Advisors choose their clients carefully because they seek long-term relationships, not sales transactions. It's not uncommon for these advisors to establish relationships that last for many decades and sometimes continue through multiple generations.

Traditional financial advisors tend to focus on transactions, rather than relationships. In fact, some are given production requirements aligned with incentives that reward them for persuading you to buy certain financial products.

FAST FACTS:

■ Men and women who plan for the future—from age 25 to 75 and with household incomes from $25,000 to $500,000—report increased satisfaction in their personal life.

■ The National Council on Aging reports that a major worry of Americans over age 75 is that they will be required to spend all of their money on long-term care.

■ **66%** of people who created an estate plan feel comfortable with their retirement security; only **37%** of those without an estate plan feel at ease.

ADVICE VS. SALES

Because they seek long-term relationships of trust that last for many years, *Objective Financial Advisors* have no agenda for advising you to buy or invest in certain financial products, such as insurance. They do give advice and help determine your need for insurance because risk management is a component of financial planning. But rather than sell financial products, they give advice and then refer you to a carefully selected expert to assist you with the details of insurance or other financial products.

FEE VS. INCENTIVE COMPENSATION

Objective Financial Advisors do not accept commissions, referral fees, or kickbacks from insurance companies or agents, attorneys, or CPAs to whom their clients are referred. In fact, many of these advisors have experts on retainer, in order to assure that their clients receive priority service from the most competent resource available.

Objective Financial Advisors are compensated with fees charged directly to the client. These fees are transparent and easy to understand.

This distinction means that *Objective Financial Advisors* are in a position to offer more trustworthy advice.

WILLINGNESS TO ASSIST WITH "PSYCHOLOGY OF MONEY" ISSUES

Strong emotions that surface when dealing with financial issues are caused by your "psychology of money." These emotions heavily influence your economic decisions. If you're married, your psychology of money can cause serious problems in your relationship.

Objective Financial Advisors are skilled at recognizing and addressing potential psychology of money challenges. Specifically, they can help you to avoid 4 common cognitive errors pertaining to money:

1. **All or nothing thinking:** This refers to habitually categorizing money situations in extreme terms. For example, something is either good or bad, or smart or dumb. In reality, financial planning is rarely so black and white.

2. **Catastrophic thinking:** The tendency to assume the worst case scenario is inevitable, as opposed to planning ahead to minimize the likelihood of the worst case scenario.

3. **Selective abstraction:** Focusing on only one aspect of financial planning while ignoring all the other factors that come into play—a common problem for those who focus too much on investment returns.

4. **Over-generalization:** Assuming that because something happened once, it will definitely happen again. We tend to overgeneralize when we lack specific knowledge about how to manage and organize our money and plan for our future.

Admittedly, this section sounds "soft" but one of the most valuable services an _Objective Financial Advisor_ can provide is to help you not fall victim to psychology of money mistakes.

FINANCIAL ADVICE AND SERVICES OFFERED BY _OBJECTIVE FINANCIAL ADVISORS_

Objective Financial Advisors offer truly integrated financial planning. Unfortunately, most financial advisors make the same statement. But few can live up to that promise when their practices are analyzed and carefully scrutinized.

One of the truest distinctions between these advisors and a traditional financial advisor pertains to how much emphasis they place on your long-term security. Traditional financial advisors tend to focus on short-term rates of return, emphasizing that they can provide you with above average returns on your investments. _Objective Financial Advisors_ by contrast, emphasize reasonable returns, but are equally focused on preservation of your assets. They guide you in addressing risks to your family's financial security, such as the area of long-term care, that traditional advisors normally minimize (unless they sell insurance).

SEVEN SPECIFIC AREAS ADDRESSED BY _OBJECTIVE FINANCIAL ADVISORS_

If money were no object, we would no doubt satisfy all of our desires. For most of us however, fulfilling all of our wants would exceed our available resources. But with careful planning and the implementation of effective strategies over many years, we can achieve results that allow us to live life as we envisioned it.

Objective Financial Advisors can best assist you in planning for your future because of their philosophy of establishing long-term relationships; the fact that they won't sell you financial products; and the fact that their compensation model is transparent and easy to understand.

They will help you create an overall strategy, using a process for setting goals, evaluating where you are with respect to your goals, developing a plan, implementing your plan, and modifying your plan as your situation changes. Even though they personally won't provide the specific services in all of the following seven areas, they'll be involved with guiding you and collaborating with the experts they've screened to assure your objectives are met.

1. **Setting financial and estate planning objectives:** This service helps you to evaluate your financial and estate planning picture. An analysis would take into consideration budgeting, emergency fund planning, credit and debt management, education funding, and insurance planning. It would also analyze estate management for those who desire to leave a legacy and/or an estate to heirs or charity.

2. **Insurance planning and risk management:** This area of financial planning addresses three general areas of risk to the overall success of your financial security: risk to your family and others you know; risk to your property; and risk to people you don't know and their property.

3. **Employee benefits planning:** Integrating benefits available to you from your place of work into your overall financial plan is crucial. This component of financial planning analyzes the advantages and disadvantages of various types of benefits, such as disability and medical insurance. It may also include evaluating optional programs offered through your workplace, including group or sponsored LTC insurance.

4. **Investment planning:** The overall goal of an investment strategy is to plan for financial independence, providing you the freedom to choose to work for money or not. An investment planning process will evaluate your personal tolerance for risk and consider vehicles such as mutual funds, stocks, bonds, and other investments.

5. **Income tax planning:** The goal of tax planning is to minimize your legitimate taxes. One of the strategies for reducing your taxes is to analyze and plan ahead for the tax consequences of investment planning, retirement planning, employee benefit planning, and estate planning.

6. **Retirement planning:** This area of planning integrates all aspects of financial and estate planning into a customized plan for financial independence.

7. **Estate planning:** This area addresses tax-efficient ways to acquire, preserve, and transfer your wealth and legacy to other parties, both during and after life. Estate planning can also address planning for incapacity due to a disability or the need for long-term care.

Objective Financial Advisors can assist you in implementing strategies in each of the above areas. While they will not directly implement every strategy, they will act as coordinators and refer you to specialists who will assist you in their area of expertise.

HOW TO LOCATE AN *OBJECTIVE FINANCIAL ADVISOR*

As mentioned many times in this book, most advisors are not *Objective Financial Advisors*. To make sure the advisor you are considering or currently working with is one, ask questions related to their investment philosophy to determine if they over-emphasize high rates of return (if so, avoid them) or preservation of your assets; whether or not they're compensated for selling products (if so, avoid them) or only charge fees for services provided; and whether or not they seem casual about the area of long-term care (if so, avoid them) or encourage you to deliberately choose your most appropriate option for long-term care.

Our firm licenses the Smart LTC Planning System to *Objective Financial Advisors* nationwide. These are America's top advisors. If you would like our assistance in locating one, please visit **www.objectivefinancialadvisors.com**.

KEY POINTS

Utilizing the Services of an *Objective Financial Advisor*

➤ *Objective Financial Advisors:*
  – Seek long-term relationships, not sales transactions
  – Have no agenda for giving the advice they provide: objectivity is their goal
  – Do not accept commissions, referral fees, or kickbacks

➤ Traditional financial advisors may focus on short-term rates of return while *Objective Financial Advisors* emphasize reasonable returns, with an equal focus on preservation of your assets.

➤ *Objective Financial Advisors* help you create an overall strategy, using a process for setting goals, evaluating where you are with respect to your goals, developing a plan, implementing your plan, and modifying your plan as your situation changes.

➤ *Objective Financial Advisors* act as coordinators by utilizing experts in specialized areas of financial planning.

Chapter 7   Seven Steps to a Smart LTC Plan™

You got to be careful if you don't know where you're going, because you might not get there.
— Yogi Berra

Who will provide your long-term care? Where will your care take place? Who will pay the bills? The long-term care industry is working to answer these questions and find solutions to the long-term care financing and delivery challenges of the next several decades. Unfortunately, solutions are not being developed in unison. This fragmentation has led to overall confusion and apathy about planning ahead for long-term care.

The solution to this problem is to develop your LTC Plan within the context of your personal and financial objectives using the guidance of an *Objective Financial Advisor*. But first, read this book, then complete the online assessment at **www.smartltcplan.com**. This will give you a head start toward ensuring that your LTC Plan is integrated with your overall financial objectives. The process involves both a logical and emotional analysis of your unique situation.

The alternative to planning ahead with this approach is to be manipulated by a *non-integrated approach* used by many insurance agents. Or, having no plan at all, causing you to default to options that expose your family to financial and emotional risks.

The following overview of the *Smart LTC Planning* process will give you a solid foundation for understanding why this is the most effective approach for planning ahead for long-term care.

SEVEN STEPS TO A *SMART LTC PLAN*™

1. Learn about Long-Term Care

Become knowledgeable about the issue of long-term care—what it is, where care can be received, and how much it costs in your area. *These subjects are discussed in Chapters 1 through 3.*

2. Evaluate the Implications of Relying on Each of the Four Resources

This is the heart of your *Smart LTC Plan*. Evaluate long-term care from the standpoint of your personal situation. How will the need for long-term care impact your family and your personal and financial objectives?

Which of the four resources available to you for paying for a potential long-term care need appear to be appropriate for your situation? *(Family, welfare, personal assets, or LTC insurance. These subjects are discussed in Chapter 4.)*

3. Narrow Down to Your Preferred Payment and Care Options

As you evaluate the long-term care resources available to you, analyze and consider each one by asking, "If I had a need for long-term care tomorrow, where would the money come from to pay for my care and who would provide my care?" For example, do you have family members who are willing and able to provide your care? If so, are you comfortable with that option? If you are, decide who specifically will provide the care. Will you move in with that person or will they move in with you?

If you are considering relying on LTC insurance, ask the LTC Planning and Insurance expert referred by your advisor to determine whether or not you qualify for coverage and to offer some ballpark premium rates.

4. Choose Your Preferred Option

The most appropriate option for your situation will become apparent after becoming knowledgeable about the issue, thoroughly understanding and analyzing your resources, and recognizing the implications for your family and your legacy if you suddenly developed a need for long-term care.

5. Develop Your Written Plan

Regardless of your choices, make sure each member of your family receives a copy of your *Smart LTC Plan*. It's vital to the preservation of your legacy and emotionally important for your family to know in advance that you haven't left this crucial area of financial and estate planning to chance. Be specific and include the location of any policies, account numbers, and funds earmarked for care, as well as the name, address, and phone number of your *Objective Financial Advisor* and LTC Planning and Insurance expert. It will most likely be these advisors and your family members who will handle the details of implementing your plan at the time you require care. Providing them with all of this information is vital.

6. Fund and Finalize Your Plan

If your written plan calls for relying on welfare, set up an appointment with an attorney familiar with the process of Medicaid Planning and the Deficit Reduction Act *(see Chapter 4: Who Pays For Long-Term Care?)*. If the plan calls for using your own assets, make sure your advisor and your family know about this choice so they know that certain monies are earmarked to pay for your long-term care needs. If your plan calls for using LTC insurance, ask the LTC Planning and Insurance expert to help you design coverage that is customized for you *(see Chapter 11: Designing the Right Coverage)*.

7. *Review Your Plan Annually*

Your plan must accomplish the objectives it was designed to achieve, both today and years from now. Long-term care is not a static issue, and any plan developed today must be periodically reviewed. Your *Objective Financial Advisor* and/or their LTC Planning and Insurance expert should review your plan at least annually to ensure it remains the appropriate solution in future years.

A Family Affair

My wife Gail and I have both faced the emotionally challenging task of placing three parents in a facility. We learned firsthand that the need for care can happen to anyone, at anytime, and without warning.

One evening, we received a call from my sister informing us that my mother was in the hospital after suffering a stroke. Mother was 84 and in relatively good health but lived alone. After the stroke, she was not able to continue living by herself, and we had to place her in a nursing home.

My wife's parents also needed long-term care. Parkinson's disease incapacitated my father-in-law, and a hip replacement that did not heal as expected left my mother-in-law disabled. He didn't know it at the time, but my father-in-law's words had a profound impact on my planning ahead for my own family. When my wife and I moved my in-laws from the home they had lived in for 40 years, my father-in-law said to me, "I sure wish we had planned for this. I'm worried that all our hard-earned savings will be used to pay for care." Both parents died in a nursing home, having used all but $2,000 of their estate.

These experiences revealed to me that a need for long-term care is emotionally and financially devastating and that long-term care is really a "family affair." Having personally traveled this journey with my own family, I realize there is no substitute for planning in advance for long-term care.

— Don Olson

	Smart LTC Planning™ Process	*Non-Integrated Approach*
Objective	• Determine most appropriate LTC Planning solution; document the plan in writing; review the plan annually	• Sell long-term care insurance
Considerations	• Overall personal and financial objectives • Insurance priorities • Personal tolerance for risk • Cost of care in your area • Your health • Affordability analysis	• Your health • Affordability of insurance • Whether or not you can be easily influenced to buy long-term care insurance
Approach	• Solutions-based planning • Consultative, educational • Emphasis placed on analyzing and documenting the best overall solution for your unique situation	• Pressure to purchase insurance • "Transaction" driven with emphasis on having you make a quick decision
Financial Professional	• An *Objective Financial Advisor*, after online assessment is completed	• Insurance agent or insurance company solicitation
Other Professional	• Recommended by your *Objective Financial Advisor* • Offers no other financial products or advice other than LTC Planning and LTC insurance • If LTC insurance is a consideration, independently licensed with several top-rated companies	• A generalist insurance agent who may have contacted you by mail, cold call, or through some other marketing "scheme" • Normally sells LTC insurance plus other types of products • Education and training may be as minimal as basic requirements needed to sell LTC insurance • May represent only one company or several companies, regardless of the companies' financial ratings
Services	• Review of plan annually for suitability, adjust accordingly • Helps with claims process if LTC insurance is part of your plan	• Contact with agent is rare following the sale • Little to no assistance at time of claim

KEY POINTS

Seven Steps to a *Smart LTC Plan*™

➤ Following the seven steps of the *Smart LTC Planning* process will result in the development of a plan for long-term care that is integrated with your family's personal and financial objectives.

➤ The alternatives to using this approach:

  – Being "sold" by an insurance agent using a *non-integrated approach*

  – Having no plan at all and exposing your family to the financial and emotional risks of long-term care

➤ At the completion of the online assessment, you will be offered the option of having your *Smart LTC Plan* reviewed annually.

PART 3

Choosing Long-Term Care Insurance As Your Option

Insurance Industry's
3 step analysis of whether or not
you need more insurance:

1. *Calculate how much*
   insurance you currently have.

2. *You need more.*

3. *We'll send someone out right away.*

— Dave Barry

PART 3:
Choosing Long-Term Care Insurance as Your Option

INTRODUCTION: HISTORY OF THE LONG-TERM CARE INSURANCE INDUSTRY

The concept of insurance dates back to 3,000 BC when Babylonian merchants began pooling their funds to reduce the economic risks of losing caravans to pirates and thieves.

This ancient idea of *pooling* the financial resources of a group to reduce the economic *risks* faced by individuals provided the foundation for today's insurance industry. Of course, the industry has now evolved to a high degree of sophistication based on well-documented statistics and probabilities.

The LTC insurance industry is in its infancy compared to most types of insurance coverage. The foundation for today's LTC insurance began in 1965 and correlates directly with the enactment of Medicare. Medicare was established to deliver health insurance for those 65 and older and for certain people with disabilities.

In addition to the newly enacted Prescription Drug benefit, there are two major parts of Medicare:
- **Part A:** Coverage for hospital and skilled nursing home care
- **Part B:** Coverage for physician's services

Shortly after Medicare was enacted, the insurance industry discovered a marketing opportunity in the Part A "skilled nursing home care" benefit. The nursing home benefit offered by Medicare only pays for the first 20 days of skilled nursing home care. Skilled nursing home insurance was invented to pay for skilled nursing home care needed beyond Medicare's 20 days of coverage. This coverage formed the foundation (and somewhat infamous reputation) of today's LTC insurance.

As the name implies, these skilled nursing home policies required that a person receive "skilled care" in order to collect policy benefits. Skilled care is uncommon, required for only the most serious types of health conditions, and is rarely needed for long periods of time.

These policies had significant shortfalls, including requirements that:
- A person first spend at least three days in a hospital prior to nursing home confinement
- A person need skilled nursing home care beyond the 20 days paid by Medicare

Because of these restrictions, the coverage rarely paid benefits and reputable financial professionals rightly advised their clients to avoid such policies.

LTC INSURANCE EVOLVES TO VIABLE SOLUTION

Beginning in the 1980s, federal and state legislators became justifiably concerned about financing health care for our aging population. As more data about long-term care surfaced, it became increasingly apparent to legislators that Medicare's skilled nursing care benefit was designed to cover acute short-term needs. Long-term care—needing care for years, not weeks—was not covered by Medicare or regular health insurance. America's aging population soon encouraged legislators to focus on supporting the development of a solution to long-term care.

By the late 1980s, laws were being passed that required LTC insurance policies to pay benefits irrespective of Medicare benefits. Further legislation required that policies cover all levels of care, not just skilled care. Over about a dozen years, long-term care insurance evolved into a viable solution for financing long-term care.

AWARENESS GROWS

Despite legislation leading to quality coverage, LTC insurance remained obscure and unpopular. For the most part, the only people familiar with the term *long-term care* were those in need of it and their families.

This lack of awareness abruptly changed in 1991. "Long-term care" became a well-known term during Bill Clinton's run for President. Clinton began his election campaign on a platform of health care reform. In speeches prior to his election, as well as during his first two years in office, he informed Americans about their lack of coverage for long-term care. In a typical speech, he would emphasize that, "Our proposed health care reform package will cover you for long-term care."

Over the next few years, we learned that long-term care is expensive. This awareness brought about an intense interest in LTC insurance as a means of funding a family's potential need for care. An industry that had previously received little public interest suddenly found itself in the limelight, with increasing demand for its once obscure coverage.

Up until the early 1990s, only 18 insurance companies offered LTC insurance. As a result of the new interest in and demand for coverage, over one hundred insurance companies entered the market. The competition for market share between insurance carriers became fierce.

New companies entering the market made some hasty decisions that benefited the consumer—at least temporarily. They reduced the overall average premium rate. Greed led to eagerness to gain dominance in the market and some insurance companies loosened their health-disqualifying restrictions, offering coverage to those with major health problems. For the first time, LTC insurance became available to those who were likely to need long-term care sooner rather than later.

GROWING PAINS FROM INEXPERIENCE

But like so many "booms," the frenzy was destined to "bust." These inexperienced insurance companies, once eager to serve an untapped market, began to feel the pains of improper pricing and underwriting. Substantial losses were incurred due to the expensive claims of policyholders who were in poor health when the coverage was issued and even poorer health a few years later. Although they continue to pay claims and are required to keep coverage in force, most of these inexperienced companies exited the LTC insurance market as fast as they entered it.

When an insurance company decides to exit a market, it becomes a major cause for concern for their policyholders. The most serious concern is that premium rates will be raised to such high levels that coverage will become unaffordable. *(Adverse Selection is explained in Chapter 17: Group and Sponsored Long-Term Care Insurance).*

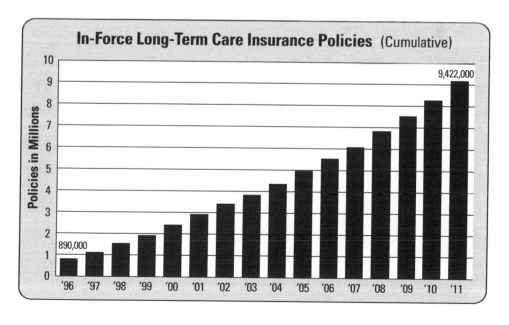

INDUSTRY MATURES

Today, a small number of quality insurance companies remain in the market-place, along with a few dozen companies that should be avoided at all costs. The quality companies are committed to the industry and are making reasonable decisions regarding underwriting, premium pricing, and more. By using the guidelines explained in *Chapter 12,* you can obtain coverage from an insurance company that will be sustainable for decades to come.

A VIABLE SOLUTION

Approximately 240,000 Americans with LTC insurance policies were paid benefits totaling $5 billion in 2011. These numbers will rise dramatically over the coming years as more Americans choose LTC insurance as their option for paying for long-term care.

Our Promise

It was a promise all five children made to our mother— that we would never put her in a nursing home. All four of her sisters had lived into their late 90s and early 100s, so the chances were high that keeping our promise could leave us caring for Mom for longer than any of us could imagine. My brother, who's a doctor, had the foresight to suggest that we look into options for paying for her care, "just in case" she ever needed it. After evaluating the four resources for paying for long-term care, we all decided that LTC insurance would be the best solution. All five children shared in the cost of the premium.

Mom was diagnosed with early Alzheimer's at 85 years old. Our normally fit and healthy mother was now frail and confused. Three of us are now taking turns having her live with us for three to four months at a time. If we hadn't planned ahead for her care, we would never have been able to afford the supplemental assistance needed to care for her. With the option we chose, Mom is able to receive care in an adult day care center for up to eight hours a day, five days a week. On weekends, we are able to hire aides to provide the respite we need from being "on duty" the full 24 hours a day.

As her disease progresses, we know that the emotional and physical demands on us and our families will be tremendous. But by planning ahead, we feel we will have the resources we need to keep our promise.

— *Michelle LaMarche*

Chapter 8 Why Some People Choose Long-Term Care Insurance

Life is pleasant. Death is peaceful.
It's the transition that's troublesome.

— Isaac Asimov

Long-term care insurance can protect and preserve a family's overall financial, emotional, and physical well-being. It pays caregivers to assist with
physically and emotionally exhausting tasks, preserving family members' energy so they can provide a higher quality of emotional support to their loved one.

In the years since long-term care insurance has gained widespread accep-
tance, several surveys have been conducted to determine the *specific* reasons
why some people choose insurance as their option for funding their *Smart
LTC Plan.*

EFFECTS OF LONG-TERM CARE BASED ON GENDER

Virtually every survey reveals that women are initially much more receptive
than men to planning ahead for long-term care. *Chapter 5* explained that long-
term care is essentially a women's issue. Almost 72% of caregivers are women.
Their average age is 48. The most likely recipient of care is the woman's
mother-in-law and/or her own mother.

Women are more affected by the need for long-term care because:
- Women outlive men by an average of seven years.
- The stress of caring for a loved one, usually her older spouse, strains a
  woman's health and many times directly or indirectly causes her to need
  long-term care.

Although caregiving provided by men is on the rise, men do not typically
feel comfortable providing the physical and emotional care needed by a family
member. So while women think ahead to the potential day-to-day physical and
emotional aspects of care, men concentrate on the more practical aspects,
including the financial consequences.

Planning ahead can relieve our family of the physical, emotional, and practical (financial) aspects of a potential need for care. Once the true impact of
a long-term care event is understood, both men and women usually become
motivated to create a plan for long-term care. This may lead to an analysis of
the suitability of long-term care insurance *(see Chapter 9).*

FAST FACTS:

- **50%** of adult children would be willing to use the money they have set aside for their own children's education to pay for a parent's long-term care expenses.

- The number of American households providing unpaid care has more than **tripled** over the past decade. Almost **72%** of these caregivers are women. The most likely recipient of care is the mother-in-law.

- The need for women to take time off work to care for aging parents has increased by **300%** over the past decade.

- **86%** of long-term care insurance policyholders know someone who has been a caregiver.

- **77%** of adults have saved for their retirement, while only **10%** have planned ahead for the greatest risk to their retirement security—long-term care.

THE MAJOR BENEFICIARIES OF PLANNING AHEAD

Our family is the major beneficiary of planning ahead because, in many cases, the person who needs care is not even aware of the need. They may be cognitively impaired or so frail that they don't understand the impact that their need for care is having on their family.

The themes of "family" and "legacy" consistently surface when people are asked why they chose LTC insurance to fund their *Smart LTC Plan.*

BENEFITS OF OWNING LTC INSURANCE

Protect Assets

Protecting assets is one of the most common reasons for planning with LTC insurance. A need for long-term care is normally paid for with cash, most often from assets accumulated for retirement. Paying for long-term care with these funds can compromise a safe and secure retirement.

During pre-retirement planning, many people purchase coverage to assure their principle will not be invaded. This protects the income their assets will later provide. Planning with insurance can allow a retired couple to more freely enjoy retirement without being concerned that a long-term care need by one spouse will alter a well-planned and secure retirement for the other spouse.

Maintain Independence

People who have firsthand experience with the challenges surrounding long-term care are the strongest advocates of planning ahead with LTC insurance. They have felt the impact of the overwhelming responsibilities that caring for a loved one brings.

The surveys reveal that many people purchase LTC insurance for themselves *after* caring for a loved one. The caregiving experience creates a strong desire to relieve their own family from having to provide them with hands-on care.

"To maintain independence" gets to the heart of the true issue of LTC Planning.

People who plan ahead in this area are the same people who have carefully planned for other risks in their lives. They are guided by a need to ensure their independence and financial security and retain as much control as possible over their lives. The thought of having to rely on children or friends for lifestyle decisions and personal care is out of the question and acts as a strong motivator for securing their legacy of independence.

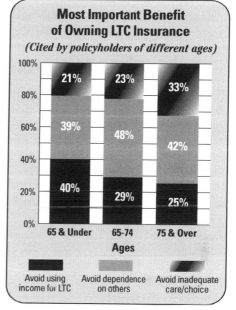

Secure High-Quality and Affordable Care

As our society ages, the demand for high-quality care will skyrocket. High-quality care may be more readily available to those who can guarantee payment with private funds—by using their own assets or by receiving benefits from an LTC insurance policy.

Long-term care insurance policy-holders may have better access to high-quality providers who wish to maintain relationships with insurance companies because they offer providers steady work and guaranteed payment. Insurance companies offering LTC insurance are beginning to locate and contract with providers who have demonstrated high-quality work and strong ethics. A provider screened and recommended by an LTC insurance company may provide better quality care than caregivers in the general population.

Maintain Current Living Arrangements

Long-term care insurance may also allow us to obtain the quality of care we need at home, without relying heavily on family and friends. Coverage may offer the peace of mind that many families need to ensure that quality care will be provided without severely altering their existing lifestyle.

About 15% of LTC insurance purchasers cite *"maintaining current living arrangement for me and my family"* as the main reason for purchasing LTC insurance.

Although some people think of LTC insurance as "nursing home insurance," the major benefit of the coverage is having the ability to remain at home or receive care in an assisted living community. This benefit may allow family members to maintain their current living arrangements and minimize disruption while still assisting with the emotional care of the loved one.

Maintaining current living arrangements is also a major benefit to families who have children with physical or mental disabilities. These families often plan with LTC insurance because their own need for long-term care could adversely affect the care of the disabled child.

CHILDREN AND PARENTS PLANNING FOR LONG-TERM CARE TOGETHER

The need for long-term care can not only deplete an inheritance, it can also affect the children's financial and career goals. To alleviate these problems, parents and children are beginning to feel comfortable discussing the issue of long-term care with one another.

RELYING ON FAMILY FOR CARE

77% Would **not** want their children or spouse to care for them.

93% Would **not** want money saved for their grandchild's education to be used for their care.

86% Would **not** want children to tap their retirement savings to pay for their care.

91% Would **not** want children to sacrifice job advancement to pay for their care.

But a survey conducted by the National Council on Aging revealed that there are distinct generational differences regarding the issue of how a parent's long-term care expenses would be funded. For example, 50% of adult children would be willing to use the money they have set aside for their own children's education to pay for a parent's long-term care expenses. This is clearly contrary to the desires of their parents. The survey revealed that 93% of parents would *not* want money set aside for their grandchildren's education to be used for their long-term care expenses. LTC insurance may offer security to both parents and children by ensuring that education, retirement income, and inheritance dollars will not be invaded.

The emotional issue of inheritance, mixed with the stress of a potential need for long-term care, may provide the catalyst for grown children to consider paying for at least some of the LTC insurance premium for their parents. This may alleviate the potential problems that can arise among siblings once a parent requires long-term care. For this reason, some children and parents are sharing in the cost of coverage.

Although inheritance and income protection are the logical reasons for having "the long-term care conversation" with parents, the surveys indicated that the primary motivation for grown children to consider sharing in the premium with their parents was the peace of mind of knowing their parents would have options for quality care. People often purchase LTC insurance because the emotional and psychological benefits of knowing their parents will be cared for outweigh the cost of the premiums.

Second Marriages

The number of people entering second marriages is growing at a faster pace than ever. In this situation, the need for long-term care by one spouse can cause problems among children of both spouses. There is a high probability that the older spouse will need long-term care services for several years because it is common for one partner in a second marriage to be considerably younger than the other. Children born of the previous marriage(s) of the younger spouse may be apprehensive that their parent's health could be affected by caring for an older spouse, or that their inheritance could be depleted paying for care for the older stepparent. Prenuptial agreements *will not* prevent the couple from having to "spend down" their combined assets before qualifying for welfare. In this case, the estate and legacy of the younger spouse are definitely at risk.

Planning ahead with LTC insurance for both partners of a second marriage can alleviate many of these concerns by assuring that neither spouse will be required to personally provide care or deplete their assets paying for their spouse's care. This allows them to protect their mental and physical health and to pass their assets down to their own bloodline.

(For guidance on how to talk with parents about long-term care, see "Breaking the Ice with Your Parents" in Chapter 3.)

Planning as a Family

The call couldn't have come at a worse time. With an infant and a newborn, both my husband and I were stretched beyond our limits. So I immediately went into crisis mode when I heard my brother say, "Dad needs help at home. He keeps forgetting to take his heart medication."

As the girl in the family, I would normally be expected to assume the role of primary caregiver. But our current situation, with two babies and demanding careers, would make it very difficult for us to provide ongoing care for Dad. Many families today are in the same situation as we are: spread across the globe with children to care for and two careers required to support the family financially.

Fortunately, we had prepared ahead of time. Years earlier, we had the "long-term care conversation" with my parents. We began by telling the story of a family we all knew who was dealing with a long-term care need. This offered us a natural opening for asking my parents if they had discussed the issue of long-term care with one another.

Our conversation was vague at first, but with the help of their financial advisor, we developed a written plan for long-term care. The plan described their deliberate choices for how their care would be provided and paid for. We then communicated the details to my siblings by providing each one with a written copy of the plan.

Initially, my brother had made comments about the whole "LTC Plan thing" being "insensitive" and "depressing." He was now expressing his gratitude for having had the conversation years earlier.

— *Liz Turner*

KEY POINTS

Why Some People Choose Long-Term Care Insurance

➤ The real beneficiary of long-term care planning is not us, it's our family—in most cases, female family members.

➤ People who plan ahead with long-term care insurance want to protect their assets; maintain their independence and financial security; secure high-quality, affordable care; maintain their current living arrangements; and/or protect their children's income, assets, and inheritance.

➤ Children and parents often plan ahead for long-term care together in order to protect the relationship they have with one another, as well as for financial reasons. Some children are sharing in the premium for long-term care insurance for their parents.

➤ Many partners in second marriages choose long-term care insurance to assure that neither spouse will be required to personally provide care or deplete their assets paying for a partner's care. This allows both spouses to remain independent and pass assets down to their own bloodline.

Chapter 9

Is Long-Term Care Insurance Right for You?

Ninety percent of the game is half mental.

— Yogi Berra

What is the optimal age to purchase LTC insurance if you are considering it as your plan for paying for long-term care? Is there a net worth high enough to eliminate LTC insurance as an option for planning ahead for long-term care? These are the questions most commonly asked by people considering LTC insurance.

The answers people receive to these questions and many others regarding the suitability of insurance are varied and usually wrong. Beware of advisors who give black-and-white answers like, "If you are younger than X or older than Y, don't consider coverage," or, "If your assets are under X or greater than Y, don't consider LTC insurance."

There is a specific strategy for determining whether or not LTC insurance is suitable for you and your family. Your best defense against purchasing coverage you may not need, or going without coverage you should have, is to consult with an *Objective Financial Advisor* (see page 59) rather than an insurance agent. Working with the advisor and the LTC Planning and Insurance expert they refer you to ensures that the plan you develop is created within the context of your overall financial objectives. Your plan may or may not include LTC insurance.

Insurance agents who sell LTC insurance using a *non-integrated approach* will debate the information in this chapter. They will tell you that you don't need to go through a "process" prior to considering LTC insurance. But the *Smart LTC Planning* process, developed over several years with the assistance and advice of carefully selected *Objective Financial Advisors*, has a proven track record as the best approach for determining if LTC insurance is right for you.

The information in this chapter is to be used only as a preliminary guide before accessing the online assessment and then having a discussion with an *Objective Financial Advisor* and the LTC Planning and Insurance expert they recommend. This chapter and the assessment does not necessarily replace the personal planning session you should have with these professionals.

FAST FACTS:

- For every year you wait to purchase coverage, your effective premium will be **12%-19%** higher.

- The percentage of people healthy enough to pass underwriting is considerably less at age 70 than at age 60.

- One in two people between age 75 and 80 will not qualify for coverage because of health conditions.

- The New York State Partnership Program recommends that you allocate no more than **7%** of your annual income to long-term care insurance premiums.

PRIORITIZING YOUR INSURANCE NEEDS

The *Smart LTC Planning* process views LTC Planning as an integral part of the financial and estate planning process. Within the seven areas of financial and estate planning explained in *Chapter 6,* LTC insurance falls specifically into the area of "risk management." Risk management is the process of deciding how to control financial risk and whether or not to transfer certain risks to an insurance company.

An evaluation of the suitability of LTC insurance will be inaccurate unless it first addresses the subject of "risk management prioritization," a process for prioritizing your personal insurance needs. This discussion may seem out of place in a book about LTC Planning, but every family has a set of insurance needs that must be analyzed and prioritized before considering LTC insurance.

The following is our list of the most important types of personal insurance, in order of priority:

1. Health Insurance: Anything can happen to our health at any time. No one in our country should be without health insurance because unexpected illnesses or accidents carry a hefty price tag. Health insurance helps a financially stable family remain secure by covering unexpected hospital and physician charges that could otherwise devastate their financial future. No other type of personal insurance is more important.

2. Disability Income Insurance: If you are working and earning an income, disability income insurance can replace a portion of your income if you become disabled and are unable to work. For people earning a working income, a risk management plan that replaces the income of the breadwinner is important. Disability income insurance protects a working income and may be an appropriate type of insurance for you..

What if you are not earning a working income? If you are retired and/or living on investment income, disability income insurance is not important. In fact, it's not even available. Disability income insurance replaces a *working income.* If you are not working for an income, this type of insurance is not applicable to you.

3. *Life Insurance:* If you are earning a working income and have children or others who are dependent upon your income, your death would mean financial hardship for your family. Life insurance is designed to relieve that hardship and is potentially your third most important type of insurance. Your financial advisor may have other reasons for advising you to purchase life insurance, such as to pay estate taxes. But if your reason for needing life insurance is other than to protect your dependents from hardship, life insurance protection should be moved to a lower priority on this list.

4. *Long-Term Care Insurance:* LTC insurance falls as low as number four on our list of insurance priorities. You should consider LTC insurance only after you and your financial advisor have analyzed your need and suitability for the above three types of personal insurance protection.

If you have not yet prioritized your insurance needs, we recommend that you address those potentially higher priority risk-management topics before continuing to learn about LTC Planning and insurance.

If you and your advisor have determined that your insurance and risk management priorities are in order, now is the appropriate time to analyze your suitability for LTC insurance.

ANALYZING YOUR SUITABILITY FOR LONG-TERM CARE INSURANCE

Determining whether or not LTC insurance is right for you involves the process of elimination. We begin by considering whether or not you qualify for coverage based on your current health. If you do not qualify, you will need to choose a different option for your plan. Analyzing the other aspects of coverage would be a waste of your time.

We then consider whether or not you can afford and are willing to pay the premium. If not, there is no reason to consider the other aspects of LTC insurance.

This process of elimination continues by analyzing other factors. As you review the information, you may decide that long-term care insurance is inappropriate for you. If you do, speak with your advisor and the LTC Planning and Insurance expert they work with to confirm your conclusion and to deliberately choose an alternative option as your LTC Plan.

REASONABLY GOOD HEALTH IS REQUIRED

Long-term care insurance is a health qualifying type of insurance; you must be in reasonably good health to obtain coverage. If your health is not good enough to qualify for coverage, no amount of premium you are willing to pay will change the fact that you're ineligible. As with all types of insurance, those who want coverage the most are often times those who can't qualify for it.

If you decide to apply for coverage, you will go through a process called *underwriting*. Underwriting is "a process of examining, accepting, or rejecting insurance risks, and then classifying those accepted in order to charge the proper amount of premium."

The LTC insurance underwriting process consists of answering questions about your health and may include a physical exam and/or request for medical information from your doctor. *(The entire underwriting process is explained in Chapter 13.)*

If you currently have certain health conditions, you will automatically be ineligible to apply for LTC insurance. The *Disqualifying Health Conditions* chart lists some of the most common types of conditions that will exclude a person from obtaining LTC insurance. This list is not all-inclusive. Even if you answer

---

LTC Insurance
Disqualifying Health Conditions

You will **not qualify** for long-term care insurance if **presently,** or during the **12-month period preceding** the application for coverage, you needed any of the following:

- Assistance with any Activities of Daily Living ("ADLs" include eating, bathing, dressing, toileting, continence, and transferring)
- Home Health Care Services
- Care in a Nursing Home or Assisted Living Community
- Use of a walker, wheelchair, medical appliance, kidney dialysis machine, or a manufactured source of oxygen
- Treatment for any of the following conditions:

  - Acute and unspecified renal failure
  - Acute cerebral vascular disease
  - AIDS
  - ALS (Lou Gehrig's Disease)
  - Alzheimer's disease
  - Chronic memory loss
  - Chronic renal failure
  - Cirrhosis of the liver
  - Congestive heart failure
  - Diabetes Mellitus with complications
  - Mental retardation

  - Multiple Myeloma
  - Multiple Sclerosis, other bone disease, or musculoskeletal disease
  - Multiple strokes
  - Muscular Dystrophy
  - Paralysis
  - Parkinson's disease
  - Schizophrenia and related disorders
  - Senility and organic mental disorders
  - Severe Emphysema
  - Transient Ischemic Attack

"no" to all of these conditions, it does not mean you will automatically qualify for coverage. Underwriting for LTC insurance is performed on an individual basis, and there may be other conditions or combinations of conditions that cause an application to be declined.

The LTC insurance industry is experiencing a trend toward more stringent underwriting. As more people collect on their coverage, insurance companies gain more insight into the reasons people need long-term care. For example, a recent study found that people who have diabetes are at greater risk for developing memory loss. This study will likely prompt other studies to explore the link between diabetes and cognitive performance.

Keep in mind that this discussion is limited strictly to your current health. If you develop a health condition(s) *after* your LTC insurance policy is issued, the company cannot cancel your policy or deny a claim due to the newly developed condition.

AGE IS A FACTOR IN UNDERWRITING

While everyone should have a written plan for long-term care, your current age may preclude your ability to plan ahead with LTC insurance. The health underwriting process is indirectly influenced by age because the older we become, the more likely we are to develop health conditions that will exclude us from obtaining coverage. For example, the chart below shows that the percentage of people who are healthy enough to pass underwriting is considerably less at age 70 than at age 60.

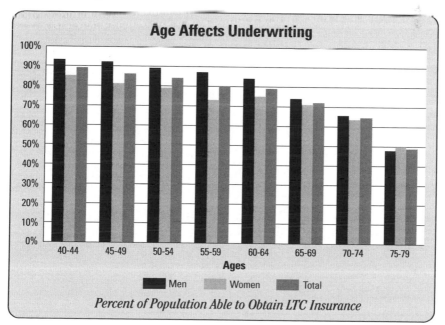

Percent of Population Able to Obtain LTC Insurance

The data also show that women are less likely to qualify for LTC insurance in almost all age brackets. This is because women often become caregivers for an older husband or elderly parents and the physical and emotional toll of providing care can have a negative effect on a person's health.

AFFORDABILITY OF LONG-TERM CARE INSURANCE BASED ON AGE

Premium rates for LTC insurance have a reputation for being high and may be unaffordable to some people. This is usually due to the fact that people postpone investigating coverage until they are too old to receive a reasonable premium rate. The younger you are when you purchase LTC insurance, the lower your premium will be for the rest of your life. For every year you wait to purchase coverage, your premium will be 8-15% higher. But this percentage does not take into account the fact that there is an overall upward trend in premium rates in the industry as a whole. When you include this upward trend in premium rates, for every year a person waits to purchase coverage, they will pay an additional 12% to 19% in premium. This means that if a 55-year-old decides to wait until they are 60 to purchase coverage, their premium will be at least 60% higher.

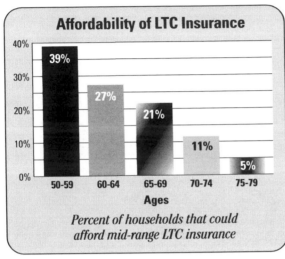

Percent of households that could afford mid-range LTC insurance

It can be a costly mistake to "wait until a certain age" to consider coverage. Some of those heeding the advice to wait until the "perfect" age will develop health conditions that disqualify them from obtaining coverage and/or will reach an age when premiums are unaffordable.

Most people are surprised to learn that the total *cumulative* premium you will pay the insurance company over your lifetime is less if you purchase coverage now, compared to waiting until you're older. For example, if a 50-year-old purchases coverage today and pays premiums until life expectancy, they will pay less total *cumulative* premium to the insurance company than a 60-year-old who purchases coverage today and pays premiums until life expectancy. In addition, the 50-year-old is more likely to qualify for coverage and be offered preferred rates based on better health.

Many people will accurately point out that this example does not consider that the 60-year-old could save, invest, and earn interest on the premium amount over that 10-year period instead of paying premiums. But it also does not consider that the 50-year-old could have a claim and collect benefits on the policy during the 10-year period. This "cumulative premium" concept is purposefully simple and is designed to point out that waiting until the "perfect age" to buy coverage can be a financial mistake.

Can you afford LTC insurance premiums at your age? As you evaluate LTC insurance, your advisor or LTC Planning and Insurance expert will provide you with a ballpark premium rate for coverage. Keep in mind that this initial figure will only be an estimate and should not be construed as your actual premium rate if you decide to purchase coverage. However, the ballpark rate will allow you to determine whether or not coverage is likely to be affordable for you.

Some people ask, "What percentage of my family's income should I allocate to LTC insurance premiums?" This will vary depending on your situation. One guideline offered by the New York State Partnership *(see Chapter 16: Partnership Programs)* recommends that you allocate no more than 7% of your gross annual income to LTC insurance premiums. This guideline should be used for general purposes only. You and your advisor should work with an LTC Planning and Insurance expert to determine an appropriate income/premium allocation based on your unique financial situation.

Are people in some age brackets better suited for choosing LTC insurance as their LTC Planning option than people in other age brackets? Yes—mainly due to insurance priorities and income. The fact that younger people tend to have insurance priorities that rank higher than LTC insurance makes them less likely to be able to afford LTC insurance, even though premium rates are fairly inexpensive.

The following is general information we have collected based on our experience regarding age and suitability for coverage. As you proceed through the *Smart LTC Planning* process, you may conclude that you fall into a different situation than the ones described.

Under age 50: People under age 50 rarely purchase LTC insurance because they fall into the category of those who have other higher-priority risks that must be covered by insurance. If they have properly prioritized their insurance needs, they may find they simply can't afford LTC insurance at this stage of their lives.

Another reason people in this age bracket rarely purchase coverage is that they are not aware of the risk; few people in this age group have had a direct experience with long-term care, so they are unaware of the need to plan ahead.

Some people in this age bracket do purchase coverage through a workplace, other group, or sponsored offering. Unfortunately, because the *Smart LTC*

Planning process is rarely utilized in these situations, there is no integration of the LTC benefits with their personal and financial objectives. If you are being offered coverage through your workplace or any group or sponsored offering, read *Chapter 17: Group and Sponsored Long-Term Care Insurance* and speak with your advisor prior to purchasing the coverage.

Between age 50 and 60: This is the fastest-growing age bracket for planning ahead with LTC insurance. People between 50 and 60 have usually met the three most important criteria for choosing LTC insurance as their planning option:

1. All their other insurance risks have been prioritized and are adequately covered.
2. They are still young enough to be in good to excellent health and qualify for coverage.
3. They can afford the LTC insurance premium.

People in this age bracket are also more aware of the need to plan ahead because they experience the highest percentage of parents or other relatives and friends in need of long-term care. People who experience a long-term care need in their circle of family and friends are highly motivated to develop a plan for long-term care for themselves and their own families.

Between age 60 and 75: People in this age bracket should strongly consider the appropriateness of LTC insurance as soon as possible. The major hurdle this age group faces is qualifying for coverage. As illustrated in the *Age Affects Underwriting* chart (see previous section: "Age is a Factor in Underwriting"), people who wait too long to consider coverage risk becoming uninsurable due to a health condition(s).

The second major hurdle for people in this age bracket is premium affordability. Premiums increase significantly at age 60 and beyond with every succeeding birthday. Coverage is likely to become unaffordable for those in this age bracket.

Most people in the 60 to 75-year-old age bracket are in one of two situations:

1. They have already investigated LTC insurance and have either purchased coverage or made the decision to plan ahead with an alternative option.
2. They are suddenly highly motivated to investigate or reinvestigate coverage for a specific reason. For example, they themselves or someone close to them have developed a health condition that has heightened their awareness of the need for long-term care. Hopefully, the person who has developed the health condition is not the same person seeking coverage. We receive inquiries on a daily basis from financial professionals with clients in this situation. Many times, the person inquiring about coverage investigated LTC insurance years

earlier but did not purchase coverage. Now, due to a decline in their health, they are motivated to obtain coverage but are uninsurable.

Over age 75: Most LTC insurance claims are submitted between age 79 and 85. For this reason, insurance companies are not anxious to approve coverage for people who have waited until age 75 or older to apply for LTC insurance.

One in two people between age 75 and 80 will not qualify for coverage due to existing health conditions. After age 80, odds are better than 80% that a person will not qualify for coverage. If they do qualify, chances are the premium will be much higher than they are willing or able to pay. If you are in this age group and want to consider LTC insurance, ask your advisor and LTC Planning and Insurance expert to analyze your situation and to possibly offer some coinsurance options that make the premium more affordable.

YOUR PERSONAL TOLERANCE FOR RISK

Your personal tolerance for risk is an important psychological consideration when determining whether or not to purchase LTC insurance. Some people have a high tolerance for financial risk, while others believe in a conservative approach and would prefer to transfer the risk to an insurance company.

People who have covered their other high-priority risks with insurance usually have a low tolerance for the financial risk of long-term care. Their philosophy is to maintain as much financial control as possible and to plan ahead for long-term care with insurance.

Your advisor will assist you in answering the following questions so you better understand your personal tolerance for risk:

- Have I consistently insured my family and myself for the proper types and amounts of insurance coverage, such as health, disability, and life insurance?

- If I have, do I tend to transfer the entire risk to the insurance company, or am I comfortable taking on some of the risk myself? In other words, should I consider coinsuring the long-term care risk?

WHY DO WEALTHY PEOPLE CONSIDER LTC INSURANCE?

If you have enough money to pay for a potential need for long-term care, should you consider LTC insurance as your plan for long-term care? Some wealthy people do.

Many people are surprised to learn that there is **no upper limit** to the amount of assets you should own before you **automatically** choose to self-insure for long-term care. Thousands of wealthy people have purchased LTC insurance even though they have the financial ability to pay for care.

Wealthy people often purchase coverage for reasons that are very different from those of the rest of the population. But one of the major reasons many wealthy people purchase coverage is to plan now for some of the major decisions their family must make in the event of a sudden need for long-term care. For example, the long-term care coordination benefit included with some LTC insurance policies can help with quickly locating quality care providers *(see Chapter 14: Submitting a Claim)*.

Many people, including some traditional financial advisors (as opposed to an *Objective Financial Advisor)*, analyze LTC insurance from a strictly logical point of view and place coverage strictly in the category of "insurance to protect assets." Although protecting assets is a common reason for purchasing coverage, many wealthy people purchase insurance for other reasons.

We've asked many high net worth individuals and families the following question about why they decided to purchase LTC insurance:

Q. **"Since you have the assets necessary to pay for long-term care without buying insurance, why are you purchasing LTC insurance?"**

Here are some of their answers:

A1. "We have always been planners. We've taught our children to plan ahead. Even though we could pay for the cost of care ourselves, we want to leave a legacy that is consistent with our lifelong philosophy of planning for the future."

A2. "All my life, I've used other people's money to succeed. For example, while some of my colleagues avoided borrowing to leverage financial opportunities, I've succeeded by borrowing and then investing that money for our future. I view the purchase of LTC insurance with this same philosophy: long-term care is a high probability risk, and if I can spend $3,000 per year in exchange for a potential $70,000 per year in benefits, I view that as leverage."

A3. "By purchasing coverage now, I lock in a lower premium rate for the rest of my life. Even though I could self-insure for all long-term care expenses today, that could change in the future. With insurance, if my investments decline in value, I won't have to worry about invading our principle to pay for long-term care expenses."

A4. "We learned about LTC insurance while we were young because we unfortunately became caregivers for one of our parents. We were also able to write off the premium on our corporate tax return. When our financial advisor and CPA analyzed the bottom line numbers, it made good fiscal sense. If one of us had a claim, we'd collect more in one month than we pay in premium for both of us in 2 years."

A5. "The 'Care Coordination Benefit' of the LTC insurance policy helps my family find quality caregivers if we have a claim. After experiencing difficulties while seeking quality care for a parent, we believe this benefit alone is worth the price of the policy."

The most appropriate LTC Planning option for you and your family is a personal choice. The option you choose has as much to do with your psychological characteristics as it does the value of your assets. People who plan ahead and achieve a successful lifestyle are more likely to plan ahead for long-term care. For some, LTC insurance makes sense even if they have sufficient assets to pay for care on their own.

KEY POINTS

Is Long-Term Care Insurance Right for You?

➤ Before considering long-term care insurance, confirm that your other risks have been prioritized based on your family's unique circumstances.

➤ The most important types of personal insurance coverage, in order, are health insurance, disability income insurance, life insurance, and long-term care insurance.

➤ If you are in poor health, no amount of premium you are willing to pay will change the fact that you're ineligible for long-term care insurance.

➤ The total *cumulative* premium you will pay over your lifetime for long-term care insurance is less if you purchase coverage now compared to waiting until you're older.

➤ Premiums significantly increase at older ages and with every succeeding birthday. Coverage is likely to be unaffordable for people who investigate insurance at older ages.

➤ Wealthy people often choose LTC insurance for reasons that are very different than the rest of the population.

Chapter 10

The Essentials of Long-Term Care Insurance

*Things which matter most must never be
at the mercy of things which matter least.*

— Goethe

If LTC insurance appears to be right for you and your family, a basic education about how this insurance works will provide you with a foundation for having a meaningful discussion with your *Objective Financial Advisor* and the LTC Planning and Insurance expert.

The essentials of LTC insurance are easier to understand when broken down into the factors that make up the coverage and impact the premium. There are seven basic factors to consider, and each factor has a direct bearing on how much you will pay for the coverage. These factors also determine when your benefits will begin, how much you will receive at the time of claim, and more.

There are also a number of optional benefits available with an LTC insurance policy. These "bells and whistles" are discussed at the end of this chapter.

SEVEN BASIC FACTORS INFLUENCING THE PREMIUM OF A LONG-TERM CARE INSURANCE POLICY:

1. How does the policy pay benefits?
2. Where can you receive care?
3. What is your current age?
4. How is your current health?
5. How much will the policy pay in benefits per day, week, or month?
6. How long will the policy pay benefits?
7. What is the policy elimination period?

BALANCING THE FACTORS

The importance of balancing and prioritizing the seven factors can't be overemphasized. Many people are in the unfortunate position of being both underinsured and overinsured, all in the same plan. This is because the agent selling the coverage did not properly balance and prioritize the factors and benefits at the time the policy was purchased. At claims time, the importance of properly balancing these factors and benefits will become evident, sometimes painfully

FAST FACTS:

- The importance of proper plan design for a long-term care insurance policy will become evident, sometimes painfully so, at claims time.

- If not for the home care coverage provided by their long-term care insurance, **60%** of policyholders would not be able to afford to remain in their homes and would be forced to move to a care facility.

- Inflation is the most serious threat to a solid LTC Plan.

so. We illustrate this with a case study in *Chapter 11: Designing the Right Coverage.*

RATING THE IMPORTANCE OF THE FACTORS

Because some LTC insurance factors are much more important than others, we have devised a numerical scale to rate the importance of each factor. We call this assignment an "Importance Rating." A rating of 5 means that the factor is very important in the overall policy design process. A rating of 1 means that it is relatively insignificant.

This rating process is heavily influenced by our opinions and experience. Some people will point out instances in which these recommendations would be detrimental at the time of claim. In this regard, LTC insurance is like all other types of insurance: If you ever have a claim on a policy of any kind, you'll wish you had purchased the maximum benefits available in every category. But we give these recommendations without the foresight of knowing whether or not you will ever collect on your policy. Based on our 24 years of policy design and claims experience, we believe the following recommendations offer a good balance between coverage choices and premium costs.

1. HOW DOES THE POLICY PAY BENEFITS?

Importance Rating: **5**

Long-term care insurance policies have three basic methods of paying benefits:

1. With the ***reimbursement method,*** also known as the expense-incurred method, you first pay the care provider, whether it be a facility or the person(s) caring for you at home. You then submit a copy of the receipt to the LTC insurance company for reimbursement. Your reimbursed amount will either be the actual amount you paid for services or your in-force "benefit amount"—whichever is less. "Benefit amount" is explained in number 5 below.

2. With the ***indemnity method,*** no receipts are necessary. The benefit paid to you is the exact amount of your in-force benefit amount, even if your long-term care expenses are less than your benefit amount.

3. With the ***cash method,*** you are not even required to incur expenses to receive benefits on a claim. You can collect your full benefit amount, even if someone cares for you free of charge.

These three methods of payment are listed in order of least to most expensive in premium cost. They are also listed in order of least to greatest amount of potential money you could receive from an insurance claim. This is where the differences end. For example, when it comes to eligibility for collecting on the policies, it's neither easier nor harder to become eligible for benefits based on the payment method of the policy.

Recommendation

On the surface, indemnity and cash method policies appear to have an advantage because they allow you to make a profit on a claim. But the reimbursement method is actually your best value because it does the most effective job of solving the true long-term care problem per premium dollar paid.

Two specific reasons to avoid policies that pay on the indemnity and cash methods are:

1. Your initial premium will be higher—significantly higher in most cases. This is because these policies make it possible for you to earn a profit on a claim by paying you a dollar amount higher than your actual costs or, in the case of cash method policies, paying you even if you do not incur expenses for care.

2. Not only will your initial premium be higher, indemnity and cash method policies will also be subject to more frequent and higher rate increases than policies that pay with the reimbursement method. This is because LTC insurance policies are placed in separate "pools" for claims experience. The method of payment, as well as other factors, determines the policy's pool. Indemnity and cash method policies are placed in a pool that is subject to paying higher and more frequent claims, making them susceptible to more frequent and higher rate increases.

2. WHERE CAN YOU RECEIVE CARE?

Importance Rating: **5**

The "type" of LTC insurance policy determines where you can receive long-term care services:

1. ***"Home Care Only"*** policies pay for care only in your home.

2. ***"Facility Care Only"*** policies pay for care only in a facility, such as an assisted living community or nursing home.

3. *"Comprehensive Long-Term Care Insurance"* policies pay for care in any setting (home and/or assisted living communities and/or nursing homes).

If a need for long-term care arises, most people want to stay in their own home to receive care. A national survey funded jointly by the Office of Disability, Aging and Long-Term Care Policy and the Robert Wood Johnson Foundation revealed that, in the absence of home care benefits provided by their LTC insurance policy, 60% of individuals collecting on their policy could not afford to remain in their homes and would be forced to move to a facility. No one wants to be forced to move from their home to an assisted living community or a nursing home simply because their policy lacks benefits for care at home. For this reason, home care benefits are an essential component of an LTC insurance policy. But in many instances, home care is not an option and a person must be moved to an assisted living community or a nursing home.

Recommendation

Since you do not know exactly where your care can be received, we recommend only the third option, the *Comprehensive Long-Term Care Insurance* policy. Only considering Comprehensive Long-Term Care Insurance is **one of the most important recommendations in this book.** Comprehensive LTC insurance offers the best value because benefits will be paid to cover skilled and non-skilled providers in your home, assisted living communities, and nursing homes. These policies may also pay for care in community-based settings, such as board and care homes and adult day centers.

Look for the words *"Comprehensive Long-Term Care Insurance Policy"* displayed prominently on the front of your policy and/or the forms and materials provided to you at the time you apply for coverage. If you see this terminology, you are considering the right type of policy because it will pay benefits in any setting. If you see any other term, such as "Home Care Only Insurance Policy" or "Nursing Home Only Insurance Policy," *do not* purchase the coverage unless your advisor and LTC Planning and Insurance expert have given you *specific* reasons for deviating from this recommendation.

3. WHAT IS YOUR CURRENT AGE?

Importance Rating:

Your **current age** will have a major impact on your LTC insurance premium. The younger you are when you purchase coverage, the lower your premium will be for the life of the policy.

When you purchase LTC insurance, you lock in your issue age premium rate for the rest of your life. This means that a 50-year-old who purchases coverage today will still be paying the 50-year-old premium rate even when they are 75 years old.

Important Clarification: Although you lock in your current age rate when you purchase LTC insurance, premium rates *can* increase after the policy is issued. But the rate increases will be on the entire "class" of policyholders, which means that everyone in your state who purchased a policy with your "policy form" from the same company will also receive a rate increase. The rate increase will always be a percentage of your current premium amount. This results in a "real dollar" rate increase that will be lower if you purchase coverage at a younger age.

When considering LTC insurance, ask about the recommended company's history of rate increases. Many insurance companies have an excellent record of premium stability, and you should consider **only** one of these companies *(for more on this subject, read Chapter 12: Choosing the Right Insurance Carrier).*

Recommendation

Although there are advantages to purchasing at a younger age, this does not mean that you should automatically purchase LTC insurance simply because you are young and can lock in a low premium rate. LTC insurance suitability is thoroughly explained in *Chapter 9* and includes such considerations as prioritizing your insurance risks prior to considering coverage.

If it is determined that LTC insurance is right for you, however, purchasing coverage at the earliest possible age is a wise decision.

4. HOW IS YOUR CURRENT HEALTH?

Importance Rating: 5

Your **current health** not only has a direct impact on the premium, but also on your eligibility for LTC insurance.

Long-term care insurance is a health qualifying type of insurance, meaning you must be in reasonably good health to qualify for coverage. While most of the general population qualifies for coverage, there are specific details about your health that will determine your exact premium, including your height and weight and whether or not you smoke.

Those in good to excellent health will likely qualify for preferred rates. Preferred rates are generally reserved for people who are average height and weight, are non-smokers, and have not experienced any negative physical or mental health conditions in recent years.

A person with minor health conditions that are well-controlled, such as arthritis without limitations, will likely qualify for coverage but will be offered a standard premium rate. The difference between a preferred premium rate and a standard premium rate averages about 15%.

If you currently have significant health problems, you may have difficulty obtaining LTC insurance. While some smaller, financially lower-rated insurance carriers might accept your application, we advise exercising extreme caution before purchasing coverage from any company that does not pass the carrier evaluation process we outline in *Chapter 12: Choosing the Right Insurance Carrier.*

Recommendation

All things being equal, consider your suitability for LTC insurance while your health is good to excellent.

5. HOW MUCH WILL THE POLICY PAY PER DAY, WEEK, OR MONTH?

Importance Rating: **5**

The **benefit amount** is the ongoing amount of money the insurance company will pay if you have a claim on the policy.

The benefit amount is the most important decision to make in designing LTC insurance coverage. It is also the most influential factor affecting the amount of your premium.

The benefit amount is expressed in a dollar amount per day, week, or month. For example, if you purchased a policy with a daily benefit amount of $150, you would collect about $4,500 per month when you became eligible for benefits, not including inflation-adjusted benefits.

Choosing the most appropriate benefit amount is imperative. It begins with knowing the cost of care in your area and using that information as a benchmark. Then, by defining your personal tolerance for risk, your personal and financial objectives, and your budget, a customized solution is developed by selecting the proper benefit amount for your unique situation. This process analyzes and determines whether to purchase coverage that will pay the full average cost of care or to coinsure by electing coverage that pays for some but not all of the average cost of care in your area.

In using a benchmark for the cost of care in your area, it's important to use the specific cost of care in your city or immediate area. Do not use the average cost of care in your state because this will not produce accurate results. For example, the cost of care in New York State can range from a low of $135 per day to a high of $278 per day.

Recommendation

Most people who purchase LTC insurance later regret that they did not purchase a higher benefit amount. Start by considering a benefit amount that covers the full average cost of care in your area. Then, if necessary, adjust the benefit amount downward based on your personal tolerance for risk and the amount of money you are budgeting for LTC insurance.

6. HOW LONG WILL THE POLICY PAY BENEFITS?

Importance Rating: **3.5**

The **maximum lifetime benefit** is the factor that determines the maximum amount of money your LTC insurance policy will pay in dollars once you have a claim and begin to receive benefits. The concept is similar to that of an accumulated savings account from which you can withdraw money. Once you have a claim, you can withdraw the daily, weekly, or monthly benefit amount explained in number 5 above. Once your maximum lifetime benefit is reached, the policy will pay no further benefits.

The maximum lifetime benefit is chosen when you apply for coverage. As soon as you collect your first dollar of benefits from the policy, it is subtracted from your maximum lifetime benefit.

You can choose a maximum lifetime benefit of as little as one year of long-term care expenses or—on the upper end—you can choose a maximum lifetime benefit with "no limit." These two examples are extremes; many in-between options exist. As you would assume, the longer the maximum lifetime benefit, the higher the premium.

The no limit choice is also known as the "unlimited benefit maximum" or a "lifetime benefit period." This option allows you to continue collecting benefits for as long as you need care, even if the care is needed for several decades or for the rest of your life.

Selecting the maximum lifetime benefit is one of the most difficult decisions to make in designing an LTC insurance policy. Accurate statistics regarding the average duration of long-term care needs are difficult to obtain. There are two major reasons for this:

1. Up until the last two decades, there has been little reason for our government or the insurance industry to keep records of how long people need long-term care.

2. When long-term care is required, people are cared for at home by a loved one—usually a wife or daughter—prior to entering a facility. Statistics regarding the duration of care received at home prior to admission to a facility are extremely difficult to obtain.

The online tools at **www.smartltcplan.com** may help you with analyzing the length of time you could need long-term care services. For example, a longer benefit period may be important if:

- There is a history of longevity in your family.
- There is a history of Alzheimer's disease or other types of dementia in your family.
- There is a history of neurological conditions, such as Parkinson's disease, in your family.

Recommendation

If you are investigating LTC insurance at a fairly young age (under 65), the difference in premium between the unlimited benefit maximum and a limited benefit maximum is fairly negligible. The unlimited benefit maximum allows you to totally solve the long-term care problem, no matter how long the care is needed.

But, if affordability is an issue, consider coverage with a limited benefit maximum. Recently obtained statistics indicate that the majority of people do not need long-term care for more than 10 years. But never choose a maximum lifetime benefit that pays benefits for less than 4 years of care.

7. WHAT IS THE POLICY ELIMINATION PERIOD?

Importance Rating:

Also known as the deductible, the **elimination period** is similar to deductibles with other types of insurance coverage, such as your automobile or homeowner's insurance. However, instead of being defined as a dollar amount, the elimination period with LTC insurance is defined in *days between the time you begin to need care and the time the policy begins to pay benefits*. For example, if you need long-term care services and you had purchased coverage with a 100-day elimination period, your elimination period would be satisfied and your policy would begin to pay the benefit amount on the 101st day of care.

The more days you are willing to pay for your care out of pocket before your policy begins paying benefits, the lower your premium rate. You can choose a variety of elimination periods ranging from a zero-day elimination period—which would pay benefits from the first day you need long-term care services—to elimination periods as high as a year or longer.

The elimination period is the most practical way to save money on your premium. An elimination period in the range of 100 days can save a significant amount of premium dollars over a lower elimination period.

In determining the elimination period most appropriate for your situation and how that translates into out-of-pocket dollars, consider two important points:

1. Your personal tolerance for risk and whether or not you believe in coin-suring a small or large amount of your potential long-term care costs.
2. The average cost of care in your area. Use this figure to calculate your out-of-pocket dollar risk for various elimination periods by multiplying the elimination period by the average cost of care per day in your area.

Recommendation

We have emphasized many times that *true* long-term care is *needing assistance for a period beyond 100 days*. Short-term care, care needed for less than 100 days, can normally be paid for without causing significant financial hardship to the person receiving the care or their family. In certain instances, a percentage of short-term care may be paid for by your health insurance or Medicare. For these reasons, always concentrate your premium dollars on covering *true* long-term care. This means choosing an elimination period of 3 months or longer.

Some people view LTC insurance as a highly catastrophic type of insurance and choose a very high elimination period—sometimes up to 2 years or longer. We caution, however, that this strategy can cause unexpected problems: If a policy's benefits cannot be accessed until years after the need for care, a policyholder and their family may be tempted to delay quality caregiving that could have been received earlier. But if this is not a concern, a high elimination period can be a practical strategy for protecting "large dollars."

RIDERS: BELLS AND WHISTLES

Long-term care insurance can be purchased with an array of extra "benefits" that can be added to the basic policy. These bells and whistles are called **riders.**

While these riders do increase your premium, they won't always add significant value to your coverage. But some are worth considering.

AUTOMATIC INFLATION PROTECTION BENEFIT

Importance Rating: **5**

The costs of long-term care services will definitely increase in the coming decades. An automatic inflation protection benefit will help hedge against these rising costs. This rider should be an essential part of virtually every LTC insurance policy.

The automatic inflation protection rider automatically raises the benefit amount of your policy each year. This rider can help to ensure that your LTC Planning objectives continue to be met.

Long-term care insurance automatic inflation protection riders normally offer a 5% simple or 5% compound inflation benefit. The compound inflation protection benefit is more costly but is the best choice because it is more realistically tied to probable inflation rates. This means that if your policy has a maximum monthly benefit of $4,000 when you purchase it, your monthly benefit will automatically rise to $4,200 per month in the 13th month of your policy. The compound inflation rider will double the benefits of your policy every 14 years. If you purchase the 5% simple inflation benefit, your benefits will double every 20 years.

You still need to monitor the rising cost of care in your area to make sure your plan is meeting your objectives. An annual review of your coverage should include a comparison of the current costs of care with your policy's latest inflation-adjusted benefit amount. If you use our online assessment, you'll be given the option to automatically receive this information annually.

Recommendation

The reason this benefit is included in the riders section of this chapter is because it is possible to purchase LTC insurance without automatic inflation protection. But inflation is here to stay, with a high probability that the inflation rate for long-term care services will be higher over time than the overall economic inflation rate.

For this reason, we recommend the following:

- Everyone who purchases coverage at age 70 and under should purchase the compound inflation protection benefit.
- If you are purchasing coverage between ages 71 and 75 and the compound inflation protection benefit adds too much to the premium, consider the simple inflation protection benefit.
- If you are purchasing coverage after age 75 and both the compound and simple inflation protection benefit riders add too much to the premium, consider increasing your benefit amount to act as a cushion against inflation. It may be more practical at these ages to purchase an additional 25% in benefit amount, for example, than to purchase an automatic inflation protection benefit. Your advisor and the LTC Planning and Insurance expert they recommend can guide you in this decision.

RESTORATION OF BENEFITS

Importance Rating:

This rider states that if you buy a policy with a "limited benefit maximum" and you use a portion of your policy benefits, the benefits in your policy will be restored if your health returns and you go without care for a specified period of time (usually six months or longer).

Recommendation

The likelihood is low that a person will receive long-term care for more than 100 days, fully recover, then later receive care again. This rider is not a good value.

NONFORFEITURE BENEFIT

Importance Rating:

This rider states that if you cancel your LTC insurance policy, a minimal amount of paid-up insurance will remain in force to slightly compensate you for premium payments paid to the insurance company. The amount of "paid-up" coverage is usually equal to the cumulative amount of premium you paid. For example, If your annual premium was $3,000 and you canceled the policy after five years, you would have paid-up coverage of $15,000. The $15,000 would be your maximum lifetime benefit. In this example, if you needed care in the future, you could collect the benefit amount up to a maximum of $15,000.

Recommendation

LTC insurance becomes more valuable the longer it's in force. Only 4% of LTC insurance policyholders cancel their policies during the first 10 years the policies are in force. This rider is not a good value.

SURVIVORSHIP BENEFIT

Importance Rating:

This rider states that if a couple have coverage with the same company and one of them passes away after the policies have been in force for a certain number of years with no claims paid on either policy, the surviving insured's policy will be "paid up"—no further premium payments would be due. The typical number of years that both policies must be in force and claim-free in order to benefit from this rider is 10.

Recommendation

This rider can be a good value if your spouse or partner is older or younger than you by at least 2 years.

SHARED CARE BENEFIT

Importance Rating:

This rider allows couples who are insured with the same insurance company to use one another's LTC insurance benefits. For example, if a couple purchases "limited maximum benefit" policies and one insured goes on claim and depletes their benefits but still requires care, this rider allows them to access the benefits of the other insured's policy.

Recommendation

We recommend first considering the unlimited benefit maximum. Following this recommendation negates the need to spend extra money on the shared care rider.

Couples who are over age 70 and cannot afford the unlimited benefit maximum may consider this rider a good value. If you are over 70 and applying for coverage with your spouse, ask your LTC Planning and Insurance expert about the feasibility of this option.

GUARANTEED INSURABILITY OPTION

Importance Rating:

This rider, also known as the "Future Purchase Option," allows you to purchase additional LTC insurance in later years without going through the health qualifying process again. This means that if you develop a health condition that would normally exclude you from purchasing additional coverage, this rider will allow you to purchase a predetermined, limited amount of additional coverage in future years.

This benefit usually offers the option to purchase additional coverage at specified intervals throughout the life of the policy. For example, the insurance company may allow you to exercise this option every two years. This offer would come in the form of a letter from the company asking if you would like to exercise the Guaranteed Insurability Option of your policy. If you elect to exercise the option, your premium for the additional coverage will be based on your new "attained age"—not the age at which you initially purchased the policy. But if you have developed new health conditions, you might be glad to have the option to purchase the additional coverage, even at the higher age rate.

Recommendation

This can be a worthwhile rider in some instances due to the increased susceptibility for developing health conditions as we age. But **NEVER** substitute this benefit for the automatic inflation protection benefit.

RETURN OF PREMIUM BENEFIT

Importance Rating:

At the time of your death, this rider returns to your beneficiary all or a portion of the premium you paid. If you collect benefits from the policy, the amount returned to your beneficiary will be reduced by the amount you collect due to a claim(s).

Recommendation

This rider adds from 25% to 40% to the basic premium. It's rarely a good value unless you're considering LTC insurance prior to age 50.

If I Knew Then What I Know Now

My mother, Millie, passed away a couple of months ago at 92 after a 12-year battle with Alzheimer's disease. Although she had been very astute in planning for her financial security, there was no way she or my sisters and I could have anticipated what the financial and emotional toll of caring for her would be. If I knew then what I know now, there are many things I would have done differently.

Twelve years is a *long* time. During that time, my three sisters and I used a variety of approaches to caring for Millie. From living with each of us, to living in an assisted living facility, and finally to needing the level of care provided in a skilled nursing home, there were unexpected health care needs that were emotionally and financially overwhelming.

During the last few years, in addition to her living in a skilled nursing facility with a one to eight staff to patient ratio, we had to hire individual caregivers to sit with her 24 hours a day so she wouldn't harm herself. The time, cost, and ever-changing health needs of our mother extended far beyond our means.

If I knew then what I know now, I would have sat down with my mother and developed a plan for her future care. If we had been aware of the potential costs and the number of years care could be needed, we would have been better prepared to handle her care—both financially and emotionally.

I don't think it's truly possible to anticipate all the special needs (and associated costs) that result from an ailing parent's need for care. However, if I knew then what I know now, I would have hoped for the best but planned, Planned, PLANNED for the worst.

— *Megan Martin*

KEY POINTS

The Essentials of Long-Term Care Insurance

➤ Seven long-term care insurance factors influence the premium.

➤ Long-term care insurance policies pay benefits under the reimbursement method, indemnity method, or cash method.

➤ Policies are specific as to where you'll receive care: home, facility, or other setting of your choice.

➤ Choose a benefit amount using a benchmark based on the cost of care in your immediate area, not the average cost of care in your state.

➤ Of all the policy riders available, the automatic inflation protection benefit is the most important benefit to purchase.

Chapter 11
Designing the Right Coverage: A Case Study

Every well-built house started in the form
of a definite purpose plus a definite plan
in the nature of a set of blueprints.

— Napoleon Hill (1883-1970)
American Writer

If LTC insurance is determined to be the best option for funding your *Smart LTC Plan,* the next step is to design coverage customized for your particular situation and personal and financial objectives. The LTC Planning and Insurance expert referred to you by your *Objective Financial Advisor* will assist you in designing your LTC insurance coverage.

DESIGNING LONG-TERM CARE INSURANCE COVERAGE

Your LTC Planning and Insurance expert will guide you through six steps:

1. **Review** the analysis that resulted in the choice of LTC insurance as your option for planning for long-term care. This analysis is a result of using the first four steps of the *Smart LTC Planning* process, explained in *Chapter 7.*

2. **Customize** the coverage. Focus on your current financial situation and personal objectives, your health, and the cost of long-term care in your area. Consider your personal tolerance for risk, which dictates your ability and willingness to pay for some of your long-term care expenses out of pocket. Taking all of these factors into consideration will result in policy benefits tailored to your unique situation.

3. **Select** the insurance carrier. Identify the insurance carriers that pass the evaluation process explained in Chapter 12 and offer options within the parameters of the customized coverage determined in Step 2. Select the most appropriate company for you and your family.

4. **Apply** for LTC insurance.

5. **Provide** a copy of your updated *Smart LTC Plan,* showing the specific LTC insurance policy benefits you've chosen, to your *Objective Financial Advisor* and to appropriate family members. If you use our online assessment, this distribution of the plan's details can be automatically generated.

6. **Review** the LTC insurance benefits at least annually with your LTC Planning and Insurance expert.

As you can see from Step 5, communication between the LTC Planning and Insurance expert and your advisor is imperative. This ensures that your coverage is fully integrated into your financial and estate planning objectives.

A CASE STUDY IN DESIGNING THE RIGHT COVERAGE

The importance of using a process such as the *Smart LTC Planning* process as opposed to a *non-integrated approach* is explained throughout this book.

To illustrate the potential results of these two opposing approaches, the following case study gives a real life example of a woman who became involved in the LTC insurance purchasing process while we were writing this book. She first worked with an agent using a traditional *non-integrated approach* and later with an LTC Planning and Insurance expert referred to her by an *Objective Financial Advisor.*

For illustrative purposes, we'll call this woman Betty Anderson. Betty was first solicited about LTC insurance by the agent who handles her automobile insurance. Consistent with a *non-integrated approach,* the agent presented her with options from the standpoint of an insurance sale, rather than from the standpoint of an integrated financial and estate planning solution. **The agent did not:**

- Educate her about the four ways to pay for long-term care
- Educate her about the cost of care in her area
- Discuss her personal tolerance for risk
- Have any knowledge of her finances and was therefore unable to assist her with an affordability analysis to determine how much she could budget for LTC insurance

The objective of the entire approach was to sell insurance, rather than to integrate the right coverage with the client's personal and financial objectives.

The agent did ask about her health, but only because this is a necessary part of the LTC insurance application process. He learned that Betty had high blood pressure; the one insurance carrier the agent represented would still offer her coverage, but only at a standard premium rate—not a preferred premium rate.

The agent attempted to persuade her to sign an application during their first conversation about LTC insurance. But she resisted, and instead, took the LTC insurance proposals to an *Objective Financial Advisor* for advice.

The advisor educated her about the need to plan ahead for long-term care and answered important basic questions about her options. After doing so, the advisor referred her to an LTC Planning and Insurance expert.

Some Facts about the Client

Before we get into the specific recommendations given by each agent and the potential implications of those recommendations, it's important to know some specific details about the client that were learned as a result of using the *Smart LTC Planning* process.

Betty is 48 years old. She is in excellent health, other than having high blood pressure, which is under good control. She is a divorced mother of twins who recently graduated from college. There is a history of longevity in her family. Her family also has a history of needing care; her father developed Alzheimer's disease and needed long-term care beginning at age 76. He received care in an assisted living facility for the final eight years of his life.

Betty owns her own employment agency, which does business as a C Corporation. Her annual income is $85,000. Her total net worth is $550,000, including liquid assets of about $125,000. She had given little thought to her tolerance for risk with regards to planning for long-term care.

The Generalist Insurance Agent's Recommendation

The generalist insurance agent focused his efforts on what he believed Betty could afford to pay for LTC insurance. He based his affordability assumption on what most of his clients who buy coverage can afford to pay.

Since the agent was not integrating an LTC Planning solution within the context of her personal and financial objectives, he did not know how to help Betty understand:

- **Affordability:** Her specific finances were not discussed, so he simply estimated that Betty could afford a premium of about $2,000 per year.

- **Cost of care in the area:** He had a general idea about the costs of long-term care, but he had no specific knowledge regarding the average cost of care in Betty's area, which is $140 per day.

- **Personal tolerance for risk:** He did not offer to assist her in determining her tolerance for risk, which would determine whether or not she should coinsure for some of the potential long-term care costs.

Other vital steps in the *Smart LTC Planning* process were also ignored, including answering one of the most important questions of all: How was it determined that LTC insurance may be the best solution for Betty? LTC insurance only makes sense if a process is used that allows a person to integrate the solution with their objectives, and if the coverage is designed based on an analysis of their personal situation.

The agent made the following plan design recommendations:

- Benefit Amount: $100 per day

- Elimination Period: 0 days

- Maximum Lifetime Benefit: Lifetime, Unlimited

- Automatic Inflation Protection Benefit: No

- Guaranteed Insurability Option: Yes

- Underwriting Class: Standard

- Policy Premiums Payable: For Life

- Annual Premium: $2,186

These benefit recommendations are imbalanced and would have resulted in Betty being both over-insured and under-insured, all in the same plan. Let's analyze each specific area:

- **Benefit Amount:** The benefit amount is the most important consideration in LTC insurance policy design. Since the agent is unaware of the average cost of care in her area, he offers no benchmark from which to recommend a benefit amount. He is recommending a low benefit amount for her situation.

- **Elimination Period:** The recommendation of an elimination period of 0 days is not appropriate because *true* long-term care begins after 100 days of care. Betty can probably afford to pay for the first few weeks or months of care herself, but neither Betty nor the agent have discussed the concept of protecting "large dollars." This would normally be discussed during an analysis of her tolerance for risk.

- **Maximum Lifetime Benefit:** The Unlimited Benefit Maximum is a good recommendation.

- **Automatic Inflation Protection Benefit:** The lack of automatic inflation protection is the most serious mistake made in the policy design recommended by this agent. The odds of needing long-term care are significant beyond age 75. But by the time Betty reaches that age, the policy would pay only a small fraction of the total costs of long-term care. The effects of inflation and the policy's lack of automatic inflation protection would cause a significant erosion to her estate at claims time.

- **Guaranteed Insurability Option:** Betty would be better advised to allocate these premium dollars elsewhere—to purchasing a higher benefit amount and choosing inflation protection, for example.

- **Underwriting Class:** Since the agent only represents one insurance company, he was unable to shop the market and locate a company that would consider offering Betty a preferred health premium rate.

- **Policy Premiums Payable:** This recommendation has Betty paying LTC insurance premiums for the rest of her life, even during her retirement years. This is appropriate in most cases. But based on the information provided by Betty during the subsequent analysis performed by the LTC Planning and Insurance expert, this approach is not optimal for her unique situation, as we'll learn below.

- **Effective Premium After Tax Write-off:** Incidentally, this agent was not aware that Betty can save $612 annually by writing off the premium as a tax deduction. This tax deduction would have been missed if she had worked only with this agent.

Potential Outcome at Claims Time

This plan design could result in enormous out-of-pocket costs for long-term care. Here is a hypothetical example:

Let's assume that Betty purchased the above coverage and followed the path of her father, developing Alzheimer's disease and entering an assisted living facility at age 76. Let's also assume that, just like her father, she ends up needing care for eight years. Between the time of purchase and the time of claim, let's assume that inflation has risen at a rate of 5% compounded annually. Let's also assume a very common scenario when it comes to whether or not people exercise the Guaranteed Insurability Option: Because of the rising costs of LTC insurance premiums during the years after her policy is issued, Betty elects not to exercise any of the options available to her with regard to the Guaranteed Insurability Option. This means her daily benefit remains at $100 per day.

Here is the cost/benefit scenario for Betty at age 76, when her hypothetical claim begins:

- The original cost of care in her area was $140 per day, but the effects of inflation and the lack of automatic inflation protection will be financially devastating to Betty at claims time. The cost of care in her area at the time of need, due to a 5% compounding inflation rate, will have quadrupled to $560 per day!

- The policy will begin to pay for care from the first day of need due to the recommendation of a zero-day elimination period.

- The 8-year duration of care equates to 2,920 days. Using the daily cost of care of $560, the total long-term care bill would come to just over $1.6 million (without adjusting for inflation during the 8 years of care).

- The policy would pay for 2,920 days of care at a rate of $100 per day. The total benefit paid by the policy for those 8 years of care would be $292,000.

- The out-of-pocket expenses to Betty would be over $1.3 million!

The generalist insurance agent might attempt to justify his recommendations by pointing out that a claim of this nature would have Betty paying only $61,000 in premiums for a return of $292,000 in benefits. But the improper coverage design would fail to meet her personal and financial objectives and would cause her to lose a large portion of her assets. This devastating impact to her financial security would be entirely due to the inappropriate plan design that often results from using a *non-integrated approach.*

The LTC Planning and Insurance Expert's Recommendation

Before meeting with Betty, the LTC Planning and Insurance expert consulted with her advisor to learn about Betty's situation and objectives. This consultation assures that the coverage will be integrated with her financial plan.

During her first meeting with Betty, the agent continued to educate her about long-term care issues that were not specifically addressed by the advisor. These issues included the specific cost of care in her area, an analysis of her personal tolerance for risk, an affordability analysis, and an analysis of her personal and financial objectives as they relate to a potential need for long-term care.

The agent supported her facts about the cost of care in the area ($140 per day) with information from various assisted living communities and home care providers in the area.

After becoming further educated about the issue of long-term care and how it relates to her personal tolerance for risk, Betty came to understand that her objective is to protect "large dollars." She was not interested in protecting relatively small amounts of money and was willing to pay for short-term care herself.

The effects of inflation were discussed, and the LTC Planning and Insurance expert emphasized that designing LTC coverage at age 48 without automatic inflation protection would be disastrous. The agent informed Betty that inflation rates for long-term care expenses were currently around 3.5%, but that this rate was predicted to double in future years and would likely average at least 5% over time.

The agent also gathered information about Betty's health but went beyond the basic information needed for an application. She asked for more specific information about Betty's high blood pressure and learned that it had been well controlled for almost six years.

Since the agent is independently licensed with a number of insurance companies, she was able to search for a company that would offer Betty preferred rates based on the fact that her blood pressure is under good control. This would save Betty about 15% in premium over the standard health rating offered by the first and only carrier represented by the agent using the *non-integrated approach.*

The agent also learned about Betty's retirement goals: She planned to work for about 15 more years and would sell her company at the time of retirement.

Determining how much she could afford to pay for the premium was an important aspect of the overall process. But even more important was creating coverage designed to accomplish the results that were important to Betty. During the affordability analysis, Betty learned that the premium for her coverage was tax deductible through her corporation. She also learned that she had the opportunity to purchase LTC insurance that could be paid up by the time she reached her retirement years.

The *Smart LTC Planning* process utilized by this expert helped Betty integrate her plan for long-term care within the context of her personal and financial objectives.

After the analysis, the LTC Planning and Insurance expert made the following plan design recommendations:

- Benefit Amount: $140 per day
- Elimination Period: 100 days
- Maximum Lifetime Benefit: Lifetime, Unlimited
- Automatic Inflation Protection Benefit: Yes
- Guaranteed Insurability Option: No
- Underwriting Class: Preferred
- Policy Premiums Payable: For 10 years
- Annual Premium: $3,856
- Effective Premium After Tax Write-off: $2,776

These recommendations offer a customized result that increases the likelihood that Betty will achieve her desired objectives.

Let's analyze each specific area:

- **Benefit Amount:** The recommended benefit amount used an accurate benchmark and pays for the average cost of care in her area today.

- **Elimination Period:** Betty saves premium dollars by choosing a comfortable elimination period. She will pay for "short-term care" (the first 100 days of care) herself.

- **Maximum Lifetime Benefit:** The policy will pay benefits for as long as the coverage is needed.

- **Automatic Inflation Protection Benefit:** Adding the automatic inflation protection benefit is the most significant difference between the recommendations given by the two agents. This benefit offers a hedge against the most serious threat to a solid LTC Plan—inflation.

- **Guaranteed Insurability Option:** This rider is not recommended to Betty because it makes more sense to use these premium dollars to purchase a higher benefit amount and inflation protection.

- **Underwriting Class:** Because this agent is independently licensed with several insurance companies, Betty received the benefit of having the agent "shop" for a company that would offer her a preferred health premium rate.

- **Policy Premiums Payable:** After learning about Betty's goal of retiring in 15 years, this agent recommended a policy that would have her paying no premiums during her retirement years. (This concept is explained in more detail in *Part 5: Questions and Answers About LTC Insurance Premiums*.)

- **Annual Premium:** Because the policy premium is payable for only 10 years instead of for life, the annual premium for this policy is higher than for the policy that requires premium payments for life. But the affordability analysis helped Betty realize that she could afford the extra premium and that it was worth the payoff of having no LTC insurance premiums in retirement.

- **Effective Premium after Tax Write-off:** Betty is informed that because she owns a C Corporation, she can deduct the premium and her effective premium rate will be reduced by $1,080 annually. Her CPA is automatically notified of the details of the coverage.

Potential Outcome at Claims Time

The hypothetical outcome of this more customized recommendation will allow Betty to receive benefits that will preserve much more of her estate at claims time. The plan is fully integrated with her personal and financial objectives and considers the future inflationary conditions that will affect her cost of care in the years ahead.

Using the same scenario of needing care for eight years beginning at age 76, this customized plan design would have the following outcome at the time of claim:

- The cost of care in her area is now $560 per day. Due to the inclusion of the automatic inflation protection rider, the policy would pay the entire cost of care.

- The elimination period of 100 days means that Betty pays for the first 100 days herself. This equates to $56,000 in out-of-pocket expenses at the onset of the need for care.

- The policy would pay benefits for 2,820 days (8 years minus the 100 days paid by Betty) for a total policy benefit payout of almost $1.6 million (not including the inflation-adjusted benefits of the coverage during the 8-year claim).

SUMMARY

By using the *Smart LTC Planning* process to customize and integrate the coverage, Betty's policy would pay an extra $1.3 million in benefits over the policy recommended as a result of using a *non-integrated approach*.

The above is a real life example of someone who worked with two agents using two opposing approaches to LTC insurance plan design. The example is for illustrative purposes only from the standpoint of the hypothetical claims.

Regardless of the choices you make, your plan should be reviewed by your *Objective Financial Advisor* or your LTC Planning and Insurance expert at least annually to ensure that it accomplishes your desired results. If you use our online assessment, you'll be given the option to have your plan reviewed every year automatically.

CASE STUDY: SUMMARY OF PLAN DESIGNS AND POTENTIAL RESULTS

	Smart LTC Planning™ Process	Non-Integrated Approach
Education and Advice	Thorough understanding of long-term care including: • Implications of relying on four ways to pay for long-term care • Cost of care in area • Analysis of personal tolerance for risk • Affordability analysis	Limited, with a major emphasis on selling LTC insurance
Integration with Personal and Financial Objectives	Major Emphasis	Minor or no Emphasis
Carrier Comparison	Several carriers	None
Underwriting Class	Preferred	Standard
Benefit Amount	$140 per day	$100 per day
Elimination Period	100 days	0 days
Maximum Lifetime Benefit	Lifetime, Unlimited	Lifetime, Unlimited
Automatic Inflation Protection Benefit	Yes	No
Guaranteed Insurability Option	No	Yes
Policy Premiums Payable	For 10 Years	For Life
Annual Premium	$3,856	$2,186
Effective Premium After Tax Write-off	$2,776	$1,574
Cumulative Premium Paid at Time of Hypothetical Claim	$35,110	$61,208
Hypothetical Policy Benefit Payout	$1.6 Million	$292,000
Hypothetical Out-of-Pocket Expenses	$56,000	$1.3 Million

KEY POINTS

Designing the Right Coverage: A Case Study

➤ Carefully consider the premium/benefit trade-off to make sure your premium dollars are used to customize coverage that is well balanced and is likely to achieve your personal and financial objectives.

➤ For the most appropriate long-term care insurance plan design, consult with an *Objective Financial Advisor* who will refer you to an LTC Planning and Insurance expert.

Chapter 12

Choosing the Right Insurance Carrier and Agent

We cannot direct the wind but we can adjust the sails.

— Vince Lombardi

Choosing the right LTC insurance carrier is the most important consideration in the LTC insurance planning process. All the other details of coverage, including benefits, premium rates, tax advantages, and more, are irrelevant if you choose the wrong insurance company. At the time of claim, the depth of commitment, integrity, and financial strength of the insurance company are what matter most.

COMMITMENT TO THE MARKET

The Introduction to *Part 3, History of the LTC Insurance Industry,* offers a chronology of the industry and describes problems that can arise if an insurance carrier enters an area of risk that they have not fully researched.

In recent years, a record number of insurance companies that entered the LTC insurance market in the mid-1990s have exited the market. Companies that exit the market must, by law, honor their commitment to current policyholders by keeping their coverage in force and paying claims.

Since an insurance company must honor its existing policies even if it exits the market, it would seem that selecting the right insurance carrier would simply be a matter of choosing the company with the best benefits and the lowest premium. However, an insurance company will only remain in markets that are profitable for the company. If a company exits the LTC insurance market, the likelihood is very high that they **did not** understand the market and, as a result, underpriced premiums and issued coverage with underwriting standards that were too liberal. To compensate, the insurance company will begin to impose frequent and sometimes substantial rate increases on its existing policyholders. These policyholders may suddenly find that what was initially the lowest premium on the market is now the highest. Since a high percentage of these existing policies have been in force for years, many policyholders will have developed health conditions that prohibit them from obtaining coverage from another insurance carrier. Their choices are now severely limited: risk paying an increasingly higher premium in the future or cancel the coverage and go without the insurance protection they had planned to use to pay for their long-term care expenses.

FAST FACTS:

- Reasonableness in premium rates is an important consideration in selecting the proper carrier. "Reasonable" means not too high or too low.

- A stringent underwriting process is an indication that the carrier will remain committed to the market.

- Consider insurance carriers that have been in the long-term care insurance market for **15 years or longer.**

- Choose one of the larger, more diversified LTC insurance carriers.

EVALUATING INSURANCE CARRIERS

History has proven that most insurance companies that enter the LTC insurance market will not remain in the market for an extended period of time. Therefore, the majority of insurance companies offering LTC insurance should be avoided. Narrow your choice of companies to those that are highly committed to the industry, have a history of excellent premium stability, and have published their claims payment history. Following are guidelines for selecting such companies.

Longevity in the Long-Term Care Insurance Industry

The longer a company has been in the LTC insurance business, the more likely they are to remain in the business. As a general rule, it is best to select an insurance company that has been in the market for 15 years or longer. Avoid companies that enter the market, exit the market, and then re-enter the market. This indicates a lack of understanding of and commitment to the LTC insurance industry.

Financial Ratings

Don't believe the myth that insurance company financial ratings are not important. On the contrary, a strong financial rating is *vital* to the future of your investment in the coverage.

You should select a company with an **A** rating or higher by the A.M. Best financial rating service. *Never* choose an insurance company rated less than **A**.

Although A.M. Best is one of the oldest and most respected financial rating services, you may also want to ask your LTC Planning and Insurance expert about a company's financial rating with one of the other rating services listed at the end of this chapter.

Name Recognition of the Insurance Company

Recognizing the name of the insurance company is another indicator that the company will remain committed to the market. Insurance companies that have built name recognition and protected a brand name over a number of decades are more likely to continue protecting their reputation. Large name brand companies rarely make short term decisions, such as entering a market without first researching it thoroughly. While small companies *may* be a safe place to invest your LTC insurance premium dollars, why take the chance? Choose one of the larger, well-recognized names in the insurance industry.

Approved as a "Partnership" Company

In *Chapter 16,* we explain that "Partnership" LTC insurance companies are superior to non-Partnership companies. Those that have been approved as Partnership companies have gone through a stringent approval process that indicates a major commitment to the LTC insurance industry. Regardless of whether a Partnership program is available in your state, narrow your insurance company selection to companies that have been Partnership approved in other states. These companies offer traditional LTC insurance in most states, and choosing one of these companies offers better odds of rate stability and a smooth claims payment experience.

Rate Increase History

Long-term care insurance premium rates can be increased on existing policies if an insurance carrier can justify the rate increase to your state's insurance department. Since policies are subject to rate increases, always ask about the rate increase history of the insurance carrier being recommended. Select one of the few insurance carriers that have done a good job with underwriting and pricing and have a record of reasonable premium rate increases.

Reasonableness in Premium

Choosing a company that has a lower-than-average premium rate could spell disaster for your future LTC insurance plan. This is one of the few industries in which shopping for the lowest price combined with the most generous benefits is not a wise strategy.

Why should you be concerned about a company with a lower- than-average premium rate? Since no company operates in a vacuum, insurance carriers with rates lower than the average market premium will raise rates substantially in future years.

Obviously, it also wouldn't be wise to purchase coverage from an insurance carrier with substantially higher-than-average premium rates. "Reasonableness in premium rates" is the best approach to selecting an insurance carrier you can trust.

Ask your LTC Planning and Insurance expert to show you premium rates from several companies. As a general guideline, the company being recommended should have premium rates that are within 15% of the other carriers that pass the evaluation process explained in this chapter.

Stringent Underwriting Process

Underwriting is the "process of examining, accepting, or rejecting insurance risks, and then classifying those accepted in order to charge the proper amount of premium" *(National Association of Insurance Commissioners)*.

For people in good to excellent health, it's best to select an insurance carrier with a rigorous underwriting process. If an insurance carrier has a conservative underwriting philosophy, it means the company's coverage is relatively difficult to obtain. Since you have maintained your good health, you should be rewarded by being insured in a "risk pool" of people who have also maintained their good health. A stringent underwriting process is your strongest indication that the insurance carrier will also be in a good position to pay your claim in the future and will be less likely to substantially raise your rates along the way.

Unfortunately, a rigorous underwriting process is not good for people in poor health, but people in poor health are very fortunate if they can obtain LTC insurance at all. Current trends in underwriting with all quality carriers indicate that people with health problems will be unable to obtain long-term care insurance in the near future.

CHOOSING YOUR AGENT

When choosing an agent to trust with your LTC insurance decisions, consider only agents who have the following characteristics:

- Compensated by more than just commissions
- Have 10 or more years of exclusive LTC planning and insurance experience
- Is willing to explain their succession plan: How they'll make sure you continue to get service after they're gone, especially at the time you have a claim
- Is independent of any one insurance company
- Is willing to provide you with names, by request, of people who have had claims and have received assistance with the claim by the agent or his/her agency
- Is willing to have their recomendations reviewed by an *Objective Financial Advisor*

FINANCIAL RATING SERVICES

A.M. Best
Ambest Rd.
Oldwick, NJ 08858
908-439-2200
www.ambest.com
Provides ratings for insurance companies. No charge for company ratings. Full written reports are available for $35 per report. Free rating information is available via the company's website.

Demotech, Inc.
2941 Donnylane Blvd.
Columbus, OH 43235
1-800-354-7207
www.demotech.com
Provides financial stability ratings for insurance companies. There is a small fee to the insurance company being rated; information is free to consumers. Information needed: insurance company name. Free rating information is available via the company's website.

Fitch
55 E. Monroe St., Suite 3500
Chicago, IL 60603
1-800-853-4824
www.fitchratings.com
Provides ratings for 1–5 insurance companies per call at no charge. Information needed: insurance company name. A fee is charged to the insurance company being rated. Free rating information is available via the company's website.

Moody's Investors Services
99 Church St.
New York, NY 10007
212-553-0377
www.moodys.com
Provides ratings for 1–5 insurance companies per call at no charge. Information needed: insurance company name. Rating information is available via the company's website.

Standard and Poor's Corporation
55 Water St.
New York, NY 10041
212-438-2400
212-208-1527
www.standardandpoors.com/ratings
Provides ratings for 1–5 insurance companies per call at no charge. Information needed: insurance company name. There is a small fee to the insurance company being rated. Free rating information is available via the company's website.

Weiss Research, Inc.
4176 Burns Rd., P.O. Box 109665
Palm Beach Gardens, FL 33410
1-800-289-9222
www.weissratings.com
Provides ratings for insurance companies. There is a $15 charge for a verbal rating (over the phone) for one company.

KEY POINTS

Choosing the Right Insurance Carrier and Agent

➤ Choosing the right insurance carrier is the most important consideration in the long-term care insurance planning process.

➤ An insurance carrier must honor all existing policies for as long as premium payments are made, even if the company exits the LTC insurance market.

➤ Only consider insurance companies that have been in the long-term care insurance market for at least 15 years.

➤ Never choose an insurance company rated less than **"A"** by A.M. Best.

➤ Choose one of the larger, well-recognized companies in the insurance industry.

➤ Narrow your insurance company selection to "Partnership" companies. These companies have made a major commitment to the LTC insurance industry, increasing your odds of rate stability and a smooth claims payment experience.

➤ Choose an insurance carrier that issues coverage with a rigorous and stringent underwriting process.

➤ Ask your LTC Planning and Insurance expert to show you the rate increase history of the company they are recommending.

➤ Choose an agent that is compensated by more than just commission; has 10 or more years experience; has a plan for making sure you're serviced after they're gone.

Chapter 13 The Application and Underwriting Process

Happiness is nothing more than
good health and a bad memory.

— Albert Schweitzer (1875-1965)

If you and your *Objective Financial Advisor* and the LTC Planning expert they recommend determine that LTC insurance is the best planning option for you, the next step is to apply for coverage. The following information explains the process for applying for coverage and what to expect in the underwriting process:

- **Complete the application.** The application includes personal information such as your name, date of birth, height, and weight. But more importantly, the application includes a series of health-related questions. The answers to these questions and the remainder of the process explained below will determine whether or not you will be issued coverage, and if so, the exact premium rate you will pay.

  The application and a refundable deposit (usually one month's premium) are submitted to the insurance company's underwriting department. The underwriting department reviews the information on the application.

- **Wait for the decision.** The insurance company may simply issue or decline the policy based on the information on the application. Although it was common for underwriting to be this simple in the past, the underwriting process today is generally more complex and requires additional steps.

- **Verification of information on your application.** A common step is a telephone conversation between a member of the company's underwriting department and the applicant to verify the information on the application. The second purpose of the call is to confirm that the applicant understands the type of coverage and benefit amounts for which he or she has applied.

- **Complete a physical exam.** The underwriter may also request a face-to-face physical. While it is becoming more routine for companies to request physical exams, most companies still limit this request to applicants above a certain age—usually 65. Physical exams may be randomly requested for younger applicants.

During the physical exam, a memory test for cognitive impairment will also be performed. This is a simple test designed to assure that a person is not already developing memory problems at the time of application.

The physical exam is paid for by the insurance company and is scheduled at a place and time that is convenient for the applicant. No disrobing is required.

- **Request for medical records.** A final step in the underwriting process may include a request for a statement of your health from your doctor and/ or a copy of your medical records.

Based on the information collected through the above steps, the underwriting department will determine whether or not to issue coverage. If coverage is issued, your health rating will be determined and this will dictate your exact premium amount. This means that the premium rate quoted by your LTC Planning and Insurance expert may be revised. The quotes provided by these professionals are based on "general underwriting guidelines," using the preliminary information you provide to them about your health. While the premium amount quoted at the time of application is usually accurate, the underwriting process must be completed prior to determining the exact premium rate.

When the policy is issued, the LTC Planning and Insurance expert will review the details of the coverage and the final premium amount with you.

You have 30 days to decide whether or not to accept the policy—this is called the "free-look period." This 30-day period begins on the date you actually receive the policy. If you decide not to accept the policy within this 30-day period, the insurance company must refund the initial deposit submitted with the application and the policy is null and void. If you agree to the conditions of the policy, including the final premium amount, the coverage will go into force.

If you accept the policy, you will be asked to select the frequency of your premium payments. Premium payments to the insurance company can be made on an annual, semiannual, quarterly, or monthly basis. Generally, discounts are available for selecting longer durations between premium payments.

If your application is declined with one insurance company, there may be options to obtain coverage with alternative insurance companies. Your LTC Planning and Insurance expert will assist you in evaluating these options.

KEY POINTS

The Application and Underwriting Process

➤ The underwriting process may involve simply completing an application, but it is more likely that additional steps will be taken prior to issuance or denial of the policy.

➤ The underwriting process must be completed in order to determine the exact final premium rate.

➤ The "free-look period" gives you 30 days to decide whether or not to accept the policy once it is approved and received.

➤ Generally, discounts are available for selecting longer durations between premium payments.

Chapter 14 Submitting A Claim

Old age is not so bad when you consider the alternatives.

— Maurice Chevalier, *Actor*

L ike all insurance coverage, LTC insurance is coverage you hope to never use. But if a long-term care need does arise, you'll certainly be thankful that you took the time to plan ahead. It will then be time to collect benefits from the investment you made in the coverage.

HOW DO YOU BECOME ELIGIBLE FOR BENEFITS?

As with all types of insurance, LTC insurance pays benefits when an "insurable event" occurs. The insurable event with life insurance, for example, is the death of the insured. The insurable event with an LTC insurance policy has to do with "needing assistance."

Specifically, there are two ways to become eligible for benefits with LTC insurance: inability to perform ADLs and/or cognitive impairment.

Inability to Perform ADLs

People who need long-term care services have lost their ability to live independently. This is often due to their inability to perform some of the activities of daily living, also known as ADLs. *Chapter 1* explained that the need for assistance with ADLs can result from the frailty of aging, a deteriorating health condition(s), or an accident.

> ## ADLs
> People who have lost their ability to perform activities of daily living, also known as **ADLs**, may require long-term care services.
>
> **ADLs include:**
> - Bathing
> - Dressing
> - Toileting
> - Continence
> - Transferring (from bed to chair, etc.)
> - Eating

The ADL list shown above presents ADLs in the order in which we typically lose them. This is the reverse order in which we learn them from birth.

At the time of claim, an ADL assessment will be performed to determine the extent of your inability to function without assistance.

Recommendation

The best policies pay benefits if you are unable to perform two or more ADLs without assistance. *Never* consider a policy that requires you to need assistance with more than two ADLs to become eligible for benefits. Especially beware of "tricky" policies that require you to lose only two ADLs to collect

FAST FACTS:

- There are two ways to become eligible for benefits: 1) The inability to perform ADLs and/or 2) Cognitive impairment.

- Care Coordinators are independent of both insurance carriers and direct care providers so they can be objective and unbiased.

- Care Coordinators recommend care based on the insured's needs and develop a plan of care that coordinates available services.

benefits for a nursing home confinement but require more ADL deficiencies to collect benefits for home care.

Cognitive Impairment

If loss of short-term or long-term memory or other cognitive impairment—such as a decline in judgment relating to safety—are severe enough that a person can no longer live independently, the policyholder may be eligible for benefits. Cognitive impairment can "trigger" benefits regardless of whether or not the policyholder is able to perform ADLs. Conditions such as Alzheimer's disease are included in this category of cognitive impairment. If this is the reason for the need for care, a cognitive assessment will be performed to determine the extent of the condition.

If the ADL and/or cognitive impairment assessment determines that you are eligible for benefits, a "plan of care" is developed. This is such an important part of the process that we explain it in detail later in this chapter under *Care Coordination*.

If you become eligible for benefits, some policies pay benefits for "homemaking services" such as cooking, cleaning, and running errands. These services fall under the category of "Incidental Activities of Daily Living," or IADLs.

Clarification: You cannot receive IADL services unless you first become eligible for benefits by either losing your ability to perform ADLs or by being cognitively impaired. LTC insurance will not pay for someone to clean, cook, and run errands for you unless you first become eligible for benefits.

POLICY EXCLUSIONS

All insurance policies contain exclusions. Exclusions are conditions or circumstances that will prevent a policyholder from collecting benefits from the policy, even if they would have otherwise qualified for benefits.

Typical exclusions found in most LTC insurance policies include:
- Treatment or services for which no charge was incurred
- Care provided or paid for by another type of coverage. For example, if Medicare or your regular health insurance paid for your care, your LTC insurance policy would not normally pay additional benefits. Remember, Medicare, Medicare Supplement insurance, and regular health insurance do not pay for *true* long-term care—care provided beyond 100 days. But if

you choose an elimination period of less than 100 days on your LTC insurance policy and one of these other sources *does* pay for your care during that time, your LTC insurance policy will not normally pay additional benefits. **Clarification: If you own more than one LTC insurance policy, you may collect benefits from both policies.**

- War or acts of war
- Alcoholism or drug addiction
- Self-inflicted injuries or attempted suicide

Beware of Mental Exclusion Clauses

Some LTC insurance policies contain an exclusion that states that mental and nervous disorders will not be covered unless the disorder is **"organically demonstrable."** Most states have banned this exclusion in policies being issued today, but be sure to read the policy exclusions section of any policy being recommended to make sure this clause is not included. **Avoid any policy that contains an exclusion of any kind for mental or nervous disorders.**

THE CLAIMS PROCESS

The claims process requires that information from three sources be provided to the insurance company: information from the policyholder, information from the provider (home care provider or facility), and information from the policyholder's physician. It is important that the information from these three sources be consistent or the claim may be delayed or denied. The last problem you and your family need to deal with at claims time is a clerical error that delays payment of your claim.

SEEK ASSISTANCE WITH THE CLAIMS PROCESS

The LTC Planning and Insurance expert who works with you when the policy is issued should be available to assist you and your family in the claims process. Prior to purchasing coverage, ask for written evidence of policyholders who have been assisted with the claims process. Ask for specific references of those who have received assistance, including phone numbers and permission to call the policyholders. If the agent cannot provide you with this information, do not do business with this person. An agent who cannot provide you with references of people who have had claims and received claims assistance should not be attempting to assist you with LTC Planning and insurance.

WHAT IF YOUR CLAIM IS DENIED?

If the claims process is handled properly, the likelihood of a legitimate claim being denied is extremely low. Most states have passed laws mandating high penalties for insurance companies that deny a legitimate claim. If you enlist the services of an LTC Planning and Insurance expert recommended by an *Objective Financial Advisor* you will have extra protection because they are aware of these laws. Their assistance with your claim will be extra assurance that the insurance company will not deny a legitimate claim.

However, if you feel a legitimate claim has been denied, contact your state insurance department to file a complaint.

CARE COORDINATION

Care Coordination is a value-added benefit that provides assistance to family members at the critical time of the need for care. Care Coordination is defined as *a service that helps manage the coordination of a person's care among all the parties involved.* These parties may include the people currently in the policyholder's circle of support: a spouse, children, other close relatives, neighbors, and friends. It may also include paid caregivers, facilities, health care practitioners, and social workers. Care Coordinators are health care practitioners who are able to assess the individual needs of a person requiring care, identify the type(s) of care needed, and assist the family in obtaining their care.

One of the major advantages of using a Care Coordinator is that you benefit from their experience in the practical aspects of long-term care. For example, the Care Coordinator is familiar with long-term care providers in the area, so their service may reduce the time it takes a family and policyholder to screen and select quality provider(s) that fit their personal needs. This allows family members to provide emotional support to the person in need of care instead of spending their time researching and interviewing potential providers.

A Care Coordinator is sometimes called a *Care Manager,* but Care Coordination should not be confused with "managed care." Care Coordinators are not "gate-keepers" to services and/or providers *(for more specifics on the difference, see "Long-Term Care Coordinators: An Interview with Health Care Experts" later in this chapter).*

The Care Coordination process involves two main steps:

1. **Conduct a comprehensive assessment.** Visit and interview the person needing care to evaluate their needs. This evaluation may include an assessment of physical and cognitive abilities, social and emotional state of mind, functional capabilities, and living arrangements. The individual's circle of support should be available during this assessment.

   This thorough assessment allows the Care Coordinator to evaluate the current resources available and link the policyholder to a full range of appropriate services.

2. Develop a plan of care. The information gathered from the assessment is used to develop a **plan of care** that describes the formal and informal needs to be addressed, the frequency and duration of care, and the cost of care. This plan of care should be developed with the participation of the policyholder, their family, and their physician.

The plan of care is a formal description that specifies the following information:

- The type(s) of care needed
- Where the care can be received
- How much the care will cost
- A recommendation regarding care providers
- Any other available alternatives

Care Coordinators may perform other services such as:

- Negotiate service provider rates
- Assist with initial claims forms
- Provide the certification (from the policyholder's doctor)
- Monitor the quality of services provided and reassess the plan of care as needed
- Develop transitional plans, such as providing assistance to a person who must be moved from their home to an assisted living community
- Document and maintain records
- Intervene during a crisis
- Manage nutrition and diet
- Coordinate bill paying services

LTC INSURANCE POLICIES ENHANCED WITH CARE COORDINATION BENEFIT

The Care Coordination benefit is included in some LTC insurance policies. Be sure to confirm that any policy you consider includes this benefit. All other aspects being equal, LTC insurance policies that offer a Care Coordination benefit are superior to policies that do not. In addition to relieving family members of the burden of trying to locate quality caregivers, the Care Coordination benefit may also result in better utilization of the benefits of an LTC insurance policy. The LTC insurance benefits may actually be extended or used more efficiently with a plan that coordinates informal and formal care.

LONG-TERM CARE COORDINATORS:
AN INTERVIEW WITH HEALTH CARE EXPERTS

Featured Experts:

- **Susan Westerman,** HIA *(Claims Manager)* and
- **Pat Pannone, RN, BSN, MPH, CMC** *(Care Coordination Manager)*
  with ERC Long-Term Care Solutions,
  Third Party Administrator, and LTCI Reinsure

This is a paraphrased interview conducted by Jesse R. Slome, CLU, ChFC, Publisher/Editor in Chief, Long-Term Care Insurance Sales Strategies Magazine, Vol. 4, No. 4 (www.ltcsales.com) and has been reprinted with permission.

SLOME: Why are some people concerned when they hear about the Care Coordination benefit of an LTC insurance policy?

PANNONE: It's natural to be concerned because many associate the LTC insurance coordination benefit with medical case management common to health insurance. Many people have experienced a hospitalization where they were introduced to someone called a case manager, who is basically a discharge planner. Or they've had contact with a case manager associated with their health insurer who is in a utilization review role. These functions are distinctly different from the geriatric Care Coordinator's role associated with LTC insurance, but it is natural for consumers to be unfamiliar or initially uncomfortable with the process of Care Coordination because of the similarity with the term "care management."

SLOME: So the Care Coordination component of LTC insurance is different. How so?

PANNONE: Long-term care insurance Care Coordination is a benefit to the insured and is stated as such in the policy. It is a consumer-focused service that links and coordinates assistance from both formal and family/community service providers. The goal is to enable policyholders with chronic functional and/or cognitive limitations to reach optimal independence for their conditions.

The coordinator has special long-term care experience and knowledge and can guide chronically ill people and their families to needed care. They are licensed health care professionals, such as a registered nurse or medical social worker. They are skilled in conducting a face-to-face "best practice" comprehensive assessment. They work with both the insured and family members to develop a needs-based plan of care, arrange services, monitor and revise the plan over time, and periodically complete a face-to-face reassessment. The coordinator who meets with the insured can also complete the certification process to establish that the individual is chronically ill.

Care Coordinators are independent of both insurance carriers and direct care providers so they can be as objective and unbiased as possible. They do not determine or pay benefits. The claim analyst interprets the policy and determines benefits based on the Care Coordinator's recommendations.

SLOME: When is the Care Coordinator engaged?

WESTERMAN: From the beginning of the need for care. Typically, a spouse or family member calls the administrator at the insurance company to file a claim. The administrator arranges for the Care Coordinator to contact the insured for a face-to-face assessment appointment. The initial assessment is typically done at the insured's home but can take place in a different setting at the request of the policyholder and family. The assessment is performed at a time that is convenient to the insured and family members who wish to be present.

SLOME: If you were paying for these Care Coordination services on an independent basis, what would it cost?

PANNONE: A geriatric Care Coordinator/Care Manager would typically charge anywhere from $1,200 to $3,000 for an initial plan, depending on the region of the country. Monitoring, and periodic on-site reassessment could cost an additional several hundred dollars a year.

WESTERMAN: And it's important to note that the cost of Care Coordination is part of the LTC insurance benefit. It's an incredibly valuable benefit for the LTC insurance policyholder.

SLOME: Do Care Coordinators know the provisions of the claimant's LTC insurance policy?

PANNONE: Not prior to the initial assessment. They recommend care based on the insured's needs, regardless of the policy benefits. But if the Care Coordinator learns there is a recommended setting or type of care not covered under the insured's policy, the Care Coordinator may assist in creating an alternate plan of care as the policy allows or find other cost-conscious alternatives to preserve the insured's resources.

SLOME: Can you share an example of how a Coordinator assisted an insured and their family?

PANNONE: One major role of the Care Coordinator is to support family caregivers so fatigue and burnout don't lead to the insured's premature move to a facility.

One case we recently worked on involved an overwhelmed 81-year-old woman caring for her husband with Parkinson's and heart problems. He had ADL deficiencies with bathing and dressing and was also memory impaired.

They didn't want to have strangers come to their home. The Coordinator recommended they consider an adult day center, explaining the available local resources that could help their situation. With supplemental help for the wife, he was able to remain living at home.

In some cases, the Coordinator might also recommend safety bars in the bathroom or an emergency response system. If the insured requires a skilled care facility, the Coordinator may arrange viable ways to have the individual return home as soon as possible to receive care.

Care Coordination is a benefit that the policyholder can receive during the elimination period. The Care Coordinator often works with the insured or family members during the elimination period to find options that could be less costly. The availability of this benefit during the elimination period is a valuable aspect of an LTC insurance policy that goes beyond the normal benefits of the coverage.

KEY POINTS

Submitting A Claim

➤ The best long-term care insurance policies pay benefits if you are unable to perform two ADLs.

➤ Policy exclusions that normally prevent a policyholder from collecting benefits include treatment for services for which no charge was incurred and self-inflicted injuries.

➤ Your LTC Planning and Insurance expert should assist in the claims process. Ask for references of people who have placed claims and received claims assistance.

➤ Care Coordination is a service that includes coordinating a person's care among all the parties involved.

➤ The Care Coordination benefit of an LTC insurance policy may help in better utilizing the policy's benefits. A coordinated plan for efficiently utilizing informal and formal care may actually extend the policy benefits.

➤ LTC insurance policies that offer Care Coordination are superior to policies that do not offer Care Coordination.

PART 4

Incentives to Purchase Long-Term Care Insurance

The aging process has you
firmly in its grasp if you never
get the urge to throw a snowball.

— Doug Larson

PART 4:
Incentives to Purchase
Long-Term Care Insurance

As our government, employers, professional organizations, and financial institutions begin to fully recognize the coming long-term care crisis, we will see more incentives to plan ahead for long-term care.

Incentives for planning ahead with LTC insurance are currently available through tax advantages; state-sponsored Partnership programs; and group or sponsored LTC insurance plans offered through employers, associations, financial institutions, and other groups. The advantages and disadvantages of these incentive programs are explained in the following three chapters.

Chapter 15

Tax Advantages of Long-Term Care Insurance

I feel very honored to pay taxes in America.
The thing is, I could probably feel
just as honored for about half the price.

— Arthur Godfrey

A year rarely passes without our federal and state governments experiencing budgetary constraints. Our country's budgetary challenges will intensify and worsen as life expectancies increase and the aging population grows.

The federal government continues to commission studies to research ways to finance the long-term care needs of our aging population, especially the 76 million aging baby boomers. But there is a pervasive fear among legislators that most Americans do not understand that public programs cannot be relied upon to pay for long-term care. Federal and state governments are actively sending strong signals that public funds to pay for the costs of long-term care will be reduced in the years ahead.

Our legislators are convinced that LTC insurance must play a key role in our country's solution to financing long-term care. Incentives are now in place to encourage more people to purchase private LTC insurance.

One incentive offered by the federal government and some states comes in the form of tax advantages for the owners of certain types of policies. Before we explain these tax advantages, it is important for you to understand the difference between policies that have been granted guaranteed tax status and those that have not.

HIPAA DEFINES TAX-QUALIFIED LTC INSURANCE POLICIES

Prior to 1997, the lack of standardization in LTC insurance policies made them difficult for consumers to understand. While many consumers purchased coverage, an equal number of people avoided LTC insurance for two major reasons:

1. Their general lack of understanding about long-term care
2. The confusing language in LTC insurance policies

Much of the confusing language was eliminated when the Health Insurance Portability and Accountability Act (HIPAA) became effective on January 1, 1997.

FAST FACTS:

- The number of people receiving Social Security benefits between now and 2050 will increase by **100%**, while the number of workers will only increase by **22%**.

- In 1940, there were 42 workers for every retiree; today, there are only 3 workers for every retiree. By 2050, this ratio is expected to be 2 to 1.

This legislation produced long needed standardization of LTC insurance policies and created tax-qualified (TQ) policies.

The passage of this act also had many positive effects on other areas of the health insurance system, but many experts believe the most significant impact of the legislation was the "legitimization" of LTC insurance. Our legislators sent clear messages that (1) our government cannot afford to finance long-term care and (2) LTC insurance will play a major role in financing long-term care.

From a practical standpoint, TQ policies are written with easier to understand language and other standardized consumer protections that are a part of every policy. For example, TQ policies offer a standardized set of criteria for determining eligibility for benefits at the time of claim.

Equally important is the standardized clarification of the tax advantages of TQ policies. HIPAA clarified that the benefits collected on TQ policies are guaranteed tax free. The legislation also grants tax deductibility of premiums under certain conditions. Prior to this legislation, the tax ramifications of collecting on a policy were unclear and premiums were not tax deductible.

NON-TAX-QUALIFIED POLICIES

It is possible to purchase LTC insurance that is non-tax-qualified (NTQ). These policies do not meet HIPAA approval and are less standardized than TQ policies. The tax treatment of NTQ policies has not been firmly established.

Since HIPAA was passed, there has been an ongoing debate in the LTC industry about the differences between NTQ and TQ long-term care insurance policies. Some people mistakenly believe that NTQ policies are less restrictive at the time of claim, but NTQ policies may actually contain language that allows an insurance company too much discretion in determining eligibility for benefits.

Due to their standardization and tax qualifications, TQ policies are superior to NTQ policies—especially for *true* long-term care. In fact, most reputable insurance companies offer only TQ policies.

If you purchased an LTC insurance policy prior to January 1, 1997, when HIPAA legislation went into effect, your policy was "grandfathered into" tax-qualified status. This means that policies issued prior to passage of HIPAA contain protections with regard to the tax advantages, even though the legislation was not in force at the time the coverage was issued. This will remain true as long as you make no *material changes* to your "grandfathered" policy. An example of a *material change* would be submitting an application to the insurance carrier to increase the benefits of your existing policy.

CAUTION: Never replace or request a modification to an LTC insurance policy you purchased in the past without first consulting an *Objective Financial Advisor (for more information about replacing an existing policy, see Part 5: Questions and Answers)*.

The remainder of this chapter will explain the specific tax advantages of TQ long-term care insurance policies.

FEDERAL TAX ADVANTAGES TAKE THE FORM OF A TAX DEDUCTION

As of 2012, the federal government does not offer a tax *credit* to owners of LTC insurance. This has been seriously debated in Congress, and a tax credit is supported by respected organizations like the American Medical Association. Most experts believe a federal tax credit will be granted in the future.

The federal government does offer tax advantages for owners of TQ long-term care insurance in the form of a tax *deduction*. Your filing status determines the rules for your federal income tax deduction.

Individuals (Non-Self-Employed) Use Form 1040 Schedule A

Individuals may deduct LTC insurance premiums as a medical expense on their federal tax return, but only if they itemize on Form 1040 Schedule A. Your total amount of medical expenses added to the allowable amount of your LTC insurance premium *(see the Maximum Allowable Premium Deduction Chart)* must exceed 7.5% of your adjusted gross income. The amount in excess of 7.5% can then be deducted from your adjusted gross income.

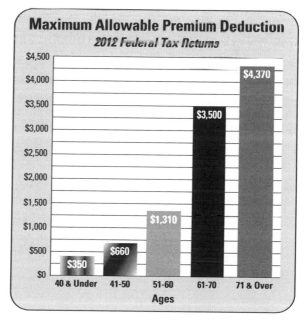

Few individuals benefit from this tax break. A person spending as much as 7.5% of their adjusted gross income on medical expenses is not likely to be healthy enough to pass LTC insurance underwriting and be issued LTC insurance. However, if a policyholder's health declines after their policy is issued and significant health care expenses are incurred, this deduction could be beneficial.

Self-Employed Individuals, S Corporations, and LLCs

Self-employed individuals, S Corporations, and LLCs have more meaningful tax advantages. These entities can deduct LTC insurance premiums for policies purchased for owners and others. For example, the company can deduct premiums paid for a spouse or other tax dependents such as parents. If the parents are not dependents, the company may still have a tax deduction if the parents are employees of the company. A tax deduction can also be taken for premiums paid for any employees' relatives.

The deduction is taken as a health insurance premium expense, so the premium is deductible regardless of whether or not you itemize deductions. Premiums *are* subject to self-employment tax.

There are limits to the tax deduction for these business entities that are based on the age of the policyholder. The *Maximum Allowable Premium Deduction Chart* shows the age ranges and amounts of deductible premium as of 2012. The IRS increases the allowable amount annually.

C Corporations

C Corporations enjoy the most favorable tax break. In fact, LTC insurance offered through C Corporations can be beneficial from a tax standpoint for both the employer and the employee. The employer can create a substantial tax deduction for the company, and if the employee has a claim, the benefits paid from the policy are not counted as part of the employee's compensation.

C Corporations can pay all or a portion of LTC insurance premiums for employees selected to receive the LTC insurance benefit. Employers who pay the premium for their employees are allowed to choose which employees receive the benefit; there is no requirement to purchase coverage for every employee.

The tax advantage to the employer is the deductibility of the *full amount* of the company's portion of the premium as a reasonable business expense. If the employee pays part or all of the premium, the employee is subject to the rules for "non-self-employed individuals" for their portion of the premium paid.

Caution: Anyone considering offering LTC insurance as a benefit to employees should first read *Chapter 17: Group and Sponsored Long-Term Care Insurance.*

No Section 125 "Cafeteria Plan" Status

Unfortunately, long-term care insurance **DOES NOT** qualify as a benefit under Section 125 "Cafeteria Plan" status. The result is that LTC insurance cannot be purchased with pre-tax dollars under an employer-provided benefits plan. This is a significant shortfall to offering LTC insurance as an employee benefit and explains why more employers do not offer coverage.

Using HSAs and MSAs to Pay LTC Insurance Premiums

Although LTC insurance premiums **cannot** be paid for with funds in an IRA or 401K plan, premiums **can** be paid for with funds in a Health Savings Account (HSA) or Medical Savings Account (MSA).

IRC Section 223(d)(2)(C) permits premiums for tax-qualified long-term care insurance policies to be considered as a qualified medical expense. This strategy *is* subject to the age based limits shown in the *"Maximum Allowable Premium Deduction"* chart.

Consult an *Objective Financial Advisor* and/or tax specialist for specific details and current rules regarding this tax strategy.

STATE TAX INCENTIVES FOR OWNING LTC INSURANCE

Unlike the federal government, some states *DO* offer a tax credit. Credits can be significant because they directly reduce the amount of taxes you owe. When a state offers a tax credit to owners of LTC insurance, the tax credit is normally a percentage of the total premium paid.

SEEK ADVICE FROM AN *OBJECTIVE FINANCIAL ADVISOR* AND/OR TAX ADVISOR

Consult an *Objective Financial Advisor* (see page 59) and/or tax advisor for a complete explanation of the latest tax ramifications of LTC insurance for your specific situation.

SUMMARY OF TAX BENEFITS FOR QUALIFIED LONG-TERM CARE INSURANCE

Type of Taxpayer	Deduction
Individual taxpayer who does NOT itemize	No deduction
Individual taxpayer who DOES itemize	• Treated the same as accident and health insurance • Limited to the actual premium paid or the eligible premium allowed (see Maximum Allowable Premium Deduction Chart) • Medical expense deduction is allowable to extent that such expenses (including payment of eligible LTC Premium) exceed 7.5% of Adjusted Gross Income
Employees (non-owners)	*Premiums paid by employee:* • Deductible if employee itemizes (follow guidelines for individual taxpayer above) • May not be paid through cafeteria plans *Premiums paid by Employer:* • Treated the same as accident and health insurance paid by employer • Deductible by employer • Total premium excluded from employee's income (not limited to eligible premium)
C Corporation	Fully deductible as reasonable business expense
Other business owners • **Sole Proprietor** • **Greater than 2% shareholder in S Corporation or Partnership** • **Limited Liability Corporation (LLC)**	• Eligible for Self-Employed health insurance deduction, which is taken "above the line" • Limited to lesser of actual premium paid or eligible LTC premium
MSA and HSA withdrawal	Eligible LTC premium is a qualified medical expense

KEY POINTS

Tax Advantages of Long-Term Care Insurance

➤ Lawmakers are concerned that Americans are not proactively planning ahead for long-term care. To alleviate part of this problem, certain LTC insurance policies offer tax advantages.

➤ HIPAA defined tax-qualified policies and standardized TQ long-term care insurance policies.

➤ Today's most reputable insurance companies offer only tax-qualified long-term care insurance policies.

➤ Policies purchased prior to January 1997 were granted tax-qualified status and will remain tax-qualified unless you make a *material change* to your policy.

➤ All federal tax advantages for long-term care insurance premiums are in the form of a tax deduction.

➤ Many states offer a tax deduction for long-term care insurance premiums; some offer a tax credit as a more powerful incentive.

Chapter 16 Partnership Policies

*The significant problems we face
cannot be solved at the same level of
thinking we were at when we created them.*

— Albert Einstein

In addition to tax incentives offered by states and the federal government, some states are offering even more generous incentives to plan ahead with LTC insurance. One program offers a promising solution to the huge challenge of providing long-term care to an increasing number of aging Americans. The "Partnership for Long-Term Care" program uses a combination of public and private money to pay for care.

The Partnership program was initially offered in four states: California, Connecticut, Indiana, and New York. Other states are continually being added to this list. If you live in a Partnership state, ask your advisor or LTC Planning and Insurance expert to offer advice about whether or not a Partnership policy is right for you. If LTC insurance is the option you are relying on for planning for long-term care, Partnership policies can be a good value.

HISTORY AND OBJECTIVES OF THE PARTNERSHIP PROGRAM

In 1986, the Robert Wood Johnson Foundation, a charitable organization instrumental in the development of the Partnership program, issued grants to 10 states to fund the study of long-term care delivery and financing. The grants were also issued to assist states in developing solutions for the problem of funding long-term care for an increasing number of aging Americans.

The outcome of this research and assistance was the creation of the Partnership for Long-Term Care program. The objectives of the program include the following:

- Cap the amount of public monies used to finance long-term care.
- Improve consumers' understanding of the challenges of financing long-term care.
- Reduce consumers' fears of impoverishment due to a need for long-term care.
- Make LTC insurance more readily available to consumers.

Standardized Requirements of Each Partnership Policy

The program requires standardized benefits that make the Partnership policies a unique consideration. Partnership policies must:

- Include inflation protection.
- Offer protection against unreasonable rate increases.
- Require agents offering Partnership policies to be specifically trained and receive Partnership certification.
- Include Care Coordination. This benefit may extend a policy's benefits and may assist the policyholder in locating care providers *(see Chapter 14: Submitting a Claim)*.
- Allow claims to be made even if the policyholder moves from the state in which the policy was issued. However, in order to benefit from the "asset protection" component of the policy (explained below), the claimant would need to move back to the issuing state, unless the state has approved a reciprocity agreement, which many have done.
- Protect you if your state decides to discontinue the Partnership Program. Your policy remains contractually protected as long as premiums are paid.

PARTNERSHIP COMPANIES ARE SUPERIOR

The Partnership program policies are private LTC insurance underwritten by a few select high-quality insurance companies. Partnership program insurance companies must go through a stringent approval process in order to offer Partnership policies. Companies willing to go through the process are making a major commitment to the LTC insurance industry, making them superior to other LTC insurance companies.

HOW DOES THE PARTNERSHIP PROGRAM WORK?

Partnership policies contain an **"asset protection"** component that allows people to shelter some or all of their assets by linking the purchase of private LTC insurance with future eligibility for Medicaid, the welfare program (Medi-Cal in California). A policyholder first uses their Partnership policy benefits to pay for long-term care expenses. If and when the benefits of the policy are exhausted, the policyholder will become eligible for Medicaid without being required to first spend all their assets on care. This allows a person who owns an LTC insurance policy certified through the Partnership program to qualify for Medicaid without having to follow the usual "spend-down" rules that impoverish most families. (Some of these Medicaid rules are explained in *Chapter 4.*) The Partnership program essentially allows you to keep some or all of your assets without requiring you to totally deplete your money paying for long-term care.

Some Partnership programs are based on a **dollar-for-dollar** model of coverage: For every dollar of LTC insurance coverage that you purchase under the Partnership program, a dollar of your assets is protected from the spend-down requirements for Medicaid eligibility. Some states offer a "bonus": Facilities in those states must offer Partnership policyholders a 5% discount off their published daily room rates.

Example of How a Partnership Policy Works

If a policyholder wants to protect $500,000 in non-exempt assets, he or she could purchase a Partnership policy with a maximum lifetime benefit of $500,000. When the policyholder becomes eligible for benefits, the insurer will pay for long-term care expenses up to $500,000, plus any inflation-adjusted benefits that have increased the coverage due to the inflation protection benefit of the policy. After the total maximum lifetime benefit is paid out by the insurance company, the policyholder could then be eligible for Medicaid benefits but maintain assets up to the total dollar benefit paid by the policy.

Some Partnership programs are based on the **total assets protection** model. With this model, Partnership certified policies must cover a certain number of years in a facility or home care, with minimum daily benefit amounts that are raised annually. Once the Partnership policy benefits are exhausted, the Medicaid eligibility process will allow the policyholder to keep an unlimited amount of assets. However, an individual's income must normally contribute to the cost of care. The New York Partnership is a total assets protection program and formally states that "the goal of the Partnership is to help people finance long-term care without impoverishing themselves or losing their life savings. At the same time, the program will help to reduce New York's massive Medicaid expenditures."

The Partnership program is a true "partnership" between the policyholder and the government because it allows participants to keep some or all of their assets, *if* they purchase a Partnership LTC insurance policy and use their insurance benefits prior to applying for assistance from Medicaid.

FUTURE OF THE PARTNERSHIP PROGRAM

The success of the Partnership program in the original states that offered it has encouraged other states to seek waivers so they can also offer partnership programs. In fact, Congress passed the Deficit Reduction Act in 2006, which is rapidly expanding the availability of Partnership programs to other states. Ask an *Objective Financial Advisor* and LTC Planning and Insurance expert if a Partnership program is available in your state.

KEY POINTS

Partnership Policies

➤ Partnership policies use a combination of private and public dollars to pay for long-term care.

➤ Under a Partnership policy, policyholders can keep some or all of their assets and still qualify for Medicaid. Long-term care insurance is used first to pay for long-term care expenses. When the policy benefits are exhausted, the policyholder may become eligible for Medicaid without having to spend down all their assets.

➤ Insurance companies that offer Partnership policies are superior to insurance companies that do not.

➤ Most experts believe that programs such as the Partnership offer the most promising solution to financing the long-term care crisis.

➤ The Deficit Reduction Act was passed in 2006 and made it possible for Partnership policies to expand into additional states.

Chapter **17** **Group and Sponsored Long-Term Care Insurance**

Success is practically guaranteed with one simple step: Carefully observe the group and do exactly the opposite.

— Earl Nightingale, *Author*

Many employers are searching for ways to help their employees avoid becoming primary caregivers in the future. In a study conducted by LifePlans, Inc., it was learned that LTC insurance benefits can reduce the caregiver workload for employees caring for loved ones. Some employers believe offering LTC insurance as an incentive will attract and retain quality employees.

LTC insurance can also be offered through an association, financial institution, or other group. Prior to considering coverage offered through your workplace, association, bank, or any other type of group or sponsored promotion, read this chapter and ask an *Objective Financial Advisor* (see page 59) for advice.

Some agents and insurance companies promote the myth that group and sponsored coverage is a good value in most situations. Although there are some people who can benefit from a group or sponsored offering, LTC insurance offered with this approach should never be *automatically* purchased. As you will learn in the "Advantages" and "Disadvantages" sections of this chapter,

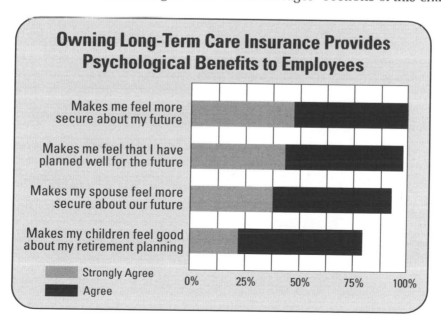

FAST FACTS:

- Long-term care insurance **DOES NOT** qualify as a benefit under Section 125 "Cafeteria Plan" status. This means that coverage cannot be purchased with pre-tax dollars under an employer-provided benefits plan.

- Individually issued LTC insurance is a better value than group LTC insurance.

you will almost always receive a better value by purchasing individually issued LTC insurance.

SIGNIFICANT SHORTFALL FOR EMPLOYERS AND EMPLOYEES

In *Chapter 15*, we explained that there can be tax advantages for employers who offer LTC insurance as an employee benefit. For example, C Corporations may deduct 100% of the premium, while the benefits paid on a claim are not subject to taxation.

We also explained that long-term care insurance **DOES NOT** qualify as a benefit under Section 125 "Cafeteria Plan" status. This means that coverage cannot be purchased with pre-tax dollars under an employer-provided benefits plan. This is a significant shortfall to offering LTC insurance as an employee benefit and explains why more employers do not offer coverage.

LONG-TERM CARE INSURANCE THROUGH YOUR WORKPLACE

Long-term care insurance could be offered through your workplace through a "true" group program or a "sponsored" program.

Group Long-Term Care Insurance

Many of the basic factors that affect the premium of individually issued LTC insurance *(explained in Chapter 10)* are also true with group LTC insurance. However, group LTC insurance has some distinct disadvantages compared to individually issued coverage.

Disadvantages of Group LTC Insurance:

1. The group market is championed by traditional insurance agents utilizing a *non-integrated approach*. LTC Planning should always be integrated with your financial and estate plan. Your *Objective Financial Advisor*, not an insurance agent, is the most appropriate professional to give you initial guidance in planning for long-term care. After giving you this initial guidance, they will refer you to an LTC Planning expert who has been screened for due diligence.

2. Group coverage usually uses a "cookie-cutter" approach to coverage: In order to encourage people to make a quick decision, insurance companies usually narrow the benefit choices to a few simple options, and enforce enrollment deadlines. This makes it difficult to obtain customized coverage that addresses your unique situation.

3. Unlike most types of group insurance coverage, group LTC insurance is usually *more* expensive, not less expensive, than individually issued coverage (when comparing identical benefits). For healthy people, an individually issued policy results in a better value than a group issued LTC insurance policy.

Group coverage is more expensive because of a problem called **adverse selection:** Group coverage allows the issuance of LTC insurance to individuals who would not normally pass typical underwriting requirements. LTC insurance sold through a group policy is normally issued with health underwriting standards that are not as strict as individually issued coverage. This results in coverage being issued to many people who are already in poor health.

Group LTC insurance is usually offered on either a **"guaranteed issue"** or a **"modified guaranteed issue"** basis. Guaranteed issue offers any employee the right to obtain coverage without being required to pass any underwriting requirements, regardless of their current health. Modified guaranteed issue means that people in extremely poor health may not qualify. But as long as a person can certify that he or she is not currently in need of long-term care services, and as long as they have not been diagnosed with a major health condition that will require long-term care in the near future, that individual will likely qualify for coverage under a modified guaranteed issue program.

Adverse selection results in a substantially higher-than-average number of claims than claims submitted by policyholders who were issued coverage with stringent underwriting requirements. Because claims are higher, healthy people who purchase coverage through the group subsidize the current premiums as well as premium increases caused by the claims of people in poor health. As a result, group LTC insurance is usually more expensive initially than individual policies and will experience higher and more frequent rate increases in the future.

> *If you are in good health, avoid group LTC insurance because:*
>
> - You are subsidizing a higher premium for those who are not healthy.
> - The poor health of many participants increases the odds of higher premium rates in the future.
> - You're limited to the narrow benefit choices of the group coverage, and pressured to make a decision due to enrollment deadlines.

Adverse selection is made worse because group LTC insurance is usually offered on a voluntary basis. The offering will be attractive to individuals who are already in poor health and know they can't obtain coverage on an individual basis. A study conducted in 2001 among buyers of group LTC insurance supported this by revealing that the number one reason for purchasing group coverage was the employee's belief that they faced a much greater than average risk of needing care. This is not good news for healthy people who participate in a group offering.

One Advantage of Group LTC Insurance:

There is one situation in which group LTC insurance is worth considering: If your health is not good enough to qualify for individually issued coverage, you may want to consider any group coverage available to you. If you decide group coverage is appropriate, ask the LTC Planning and Insurance expert referred by an *Objective Financial Advisor* for assistance in selecting the most appropriate benefits within the "cookie-cutter" group policy options being offered. This will result in coverage that is as close as possible to a customized solution.

When evaluating the coverage offered by the group, request information about the financial rating of the insurance company issuing the coverage. As explained in *Chapter 12,* it's imperative to have coverage with a company rated **A** or higher with A.M. Best. An insurance company with a lower rating that offers a guaranteed issue or modified guaranteed issue group LTC insurance policy has higher odds of experiencing financial problems. This could compromise your ability to collect policy benefits after paying the premiums for a number of years. Just as detrimental, such carriers are likely to impose such frequent and substantial rate increases that the coverage becomes unaffordable.

Sponsored Long-Term Care Insurance

Sponsored LTC insurance may be offered through a variety of entities, including your employer; a financial institution such as a credit union, bank, or stock brokerage firm; your local Chamber of Commerce; a senior or retirement association; or some other group or professional organization to which you belong. Insurance companies offer sponsored LTC insurance policies that are marketed by agents or through marketing campaigns, such as advertisements, direct mail, phone solicitations, websites, or email.

Sponsored LTC insurance is a better value for healthy people than group LTC insurance. Since they use the same stringent underwriting guidelines as individually issued policies, sponsored programs are not likely to experience the adverse selection problems of group LTC insurance programs. But sponsored offerings almost always fail to offer the best overall value.

Disadvantages of Sponsored LTC Insurance:

1. There is only one insurance company sponsoring the program, so you're limited to the narrow coverage options offered by that company. A plan offered by another carrier may give you more appropriate coverage options for your unique situation.

2. Some sponsored programs may advertise a 5%-10% discount, but this discounted premium could be a marketing gimmick. In reality, the discounted premium may be higher than the normal premium rate offered by an alternative insurance company. Ask your LTC Planning and Insurance expert for premium and benefit comparisons among several insurance carriers prior to considering any sponsored offering.

3. As with group coverage, sponsored offerings are usually promoted by insurance agents who sell LTC insurance using a *non-integrated approach*, instead of the *Smart LTC Planning* process.

4. If an agent is not involved, it means that the insurance company is selling coverage directly by phone, internet, or mail. Buying directly from the carrier saves no money and leaves you on your own to deal directly with the company at the time of claim, instead of having an advocate to assist you with your claim.

One Advantage of Sponsored LTC Insurance:

There is one situation in which sponsored LTC insurance is worth considering: when the employer, association, or other organization uses the services of an *Objective Financial Advisor* and their LTC Planning and Insurance expert. This scenario may offer the best of all worlds:

- The ability to choose coverage among several insurance carriers

- The advantage of using the *Smart LTC Planning* process, integrating the coverage with your personal and financial objectives

- The possibility of receiving a 5%-10% discount on the premium

GROUP AND SPONSORED LTC INSURANCE

	ADVANTAGES	DISADVANTAGES
GROUP	Guaranteed/modified issue coverage may allow people in poor health to obtain long-term care insurance when they would otherwise not qualify for an individually issued policy	Long-term care insurance sold with a *non-integrated approach.* Coverage is not normally integrated with your personal and financial objectives **Adverse selection** allows those in poor health to obtain coverage, resulting in higher initial premiums for those in good health. This also raises the risk of increasingly higher premium rates in the future Limited to the coverage options offered by the insurance company offering the coverage. This eliminates the opportunity to compare coverage and premium rates among various carriers
SPONSORED	Possible discount of 5%–10% Working with an *Objective Financial Advisor* and their LTC Planning and Insurance expert may offer additional advantages: • Choice of multiple carriers • *Smart LTC Plan* and policy design developed within the context of your personal and financial objectives • Assistance at time of claim	Long-term care insurance sold with a *non-integrated approach.* Coverage is not normally integrated with your personal and financial objectives Even with a discount, premium may be higher than with coverage offered by an alternative carrier Limited to the coverage options offered by the insurance company offering the coverage. This eliminates the opportunity to compare coverage and premium rates among various carriers

KEY POINTS

Group and Sponsored Long-Term Care Insurance

➤ Group long-term care insurance is typically issued with lenient underwriting standards, causing healthy policyholders to subsidize the premium of people in poor health.

➤ Group plans attract people who are already in poor health and cannot obtain long-term care insurance any other way.

➤ **Adverse selection** results when the group of policyholders includes too many people in poor health and too few in excellent health. As a result, the insurance company has a higher than average number of claims and charges higher premium rates, with high odds of increasingly higher premium rates in the future.

➤ Sponsored long-term care insurance policies can be offered through employers, retirement associations, financial institutions, and other groups.

➤ Sponsored policies are superior to true group policies because they are individually issued and use a stringent underwriting process, but they usually fail to offer the best overall value. The exception to this is a sponsored program that enlists the services of an *Objective Financial Advisor* and their LTC Planning and Insurance expert.

PART 5

Questions & Answers about Long-Term Care Insurance

*Never let your schoolin' get
in the way of your education.*

— Mark Twain

PART 5:
Questions & Answers about
Long-Term Care Insurance

Over the years, we have been asked thousands of questions about long-term care insurance. We've answered the majority of those questions in the previous pages, but some questions were difficult to incorporate into the general text. These miscellaneous questions will be answered in this section.

GENERAL QUESTIONS ABOUT LTC INSURANCE

Q. A financial advisor on television continuously states that LTC insurance should only be considered by people over a certain age. This advisor has used two ages as "ideal" for purchasing coverage: 54 and 59. Is she right?

A. No. This subject is discussed in several areas of this book, and comprehensively in *Chapter 9*. This erroneous advice is one of the most prevalent and dangerous myths in LTC Planning.

Whether or not to purchase LTC insurance has nothing to do with your age. It has to do with whether you have prioritized your insurance needs, whether you can afford the LTC insurance premium, your tolerance for risk, and other factors.

There are a number of reasons why blanket advice to wait until a "perfect age" before considering LTC insurance is dangerous. The two major reasons are:

1. Long-term care insurance premiums rise with each year a person waits to purchase coverage and are also on the rise in the industry in general.

2. While waiting until the "perfect age" to purchase coverage, many people will become uninsurable, and some may even begin needing long-term care.

Q. Is there an age at which LTC insurance becomes unattainable?

A. Some insurance companies issue coverage up until age 84. However, most carriers restrict the benefit choices for applicants over age 79. This means that even if the applicant qualifies for coverage, the benefit options may be very narrow. LTC insurance is rarely issued at older ages, due to the likelihood of being ineligible due to poor health and unaffordable premiums.

Q. *Should a person who would qualify for Medicaid, the welfare program, purchase LTC insurance?*

A. No. People who qualify for Medicaid do not need LTC insurance because the welfare system will pay for their care. It would be unethical for an insurance agent to solicit or an insurance company to sell an LTC insurance policy to an individual who qualifies for Medicaid benefits.

Q. *What is the difference between "guaranteed renewable" and "non-cancelable" LTC insurance?*

A. Guaranteed renewable policies guarantee that the policy must be renewed for life as long as premium payments are paid on time. However, the insurance company reserves the right to increase the premium as long as the premium increase is implemented on a class basis, not an individual basis.

A non-cancelable policy would guarantee that (1) the policy is renewable for life if premium payments are paid on time, and (2) the insurance company can never increase the premium rates, even on a class basis.

Although insurance companies have offered non-cancelable policies in the past, there are none available today. You may, however, purchase a rider that guarantees your premium rate will not be increased for a specified number of years. But the best strategy for avoiding frequent rate increases is to follow the advice given in *Chapter 12: Choosing the Right Insurance Carrier and Agent.*

Q. *Can a person purchase an LTC insurance policy for a parent or someone else without them knowing that the coverage has been purchased?*

A. No. The person who will be insured must consent to the coverage by signing an application. They must also be fully aware of the purpose of the application, understand the policy benefits, and understand the underwriting process.

However, a person may pay the premium for another person. In many cases, children pay the premium for their parents' LTC insurance coverage. *(This is explained in more detail in Chapter 8: Why Some People Choose Long-Term Care Insurance.)*

Q. *If a person already owns an LTC insurance policy, should they ever replace the policy?*

A. The decision of whether or not to replace a current policy should be taken very seriously and analyzed by an *Objective Financial Advisor* and their LTC Planning and Insurance expert. In most cases, you have more to lose than gain by replacing an existing policy, but each situation is unique and should be analyzed by considering the following questions:

- Is your current insurance carrier financially stable and committed to the LTC insurance industry? Do they increase your premium rates frequently?

- Has your health changed for the worse since you purchased the policy? If so, you may not qualify if you applied for coverage today.

- How long ago was the policy purchased? A policy purchased several years ago probably has a fairly low premium compared to the premium of newly issued coverage today. This may be true even if your current carrier has increased your premium rate.

Q. *Is it important to work with an LTC Planning and Insurance expert who is recommended by an Objective Financial Advisor?*

A. It's *absolutely* essential. In addition to being thoroughly screened for due diligence, these experts are independent of any single insurance company. Never work with an agent who represents only one company. They will have too strong of an allegiance to that company and not necessarily to you.

Q. *Is there a safety net in place for policyholders who have coverage with an insurance company that becomes insolvent?*

A. *Chapter 12* explains the importance of carefully choosing an insurance carrier. By following the guidelines explained in that chapter, your chances of having to face this type of situation are greatly reduced.

But there are protections in place if the company insuring you becomes insolvent. Most states operate Guarantee Associations designed to become the insurer for policyholders who have purchased coverage from carriers that become insolvent. The specific benefits of Guarantee Associations and the way they operate vary from state to state. Contact your state's insurance department for more specifics about the availability of a Guarantee Association in your state.

Q. *What happens if I buy an LTC insurance policy and the insurance company later decides to stop offering LTC insurance to future applicants?*

A. All individually issued policies sold today are guaranteed renewable. This means that the company cannot cancel your policy as long as you pay your premium on time. This is true even if the company decides to no longer offer coverage to future applicants.

Policies issued in earlier years and group coverage may or may not be "guaranteed renewable" and thus may be cancelable. If you currently own an LTC insurance policy, look for the words **"Guaranteed Renewable"** on the front of the policy. Other terminology such as "Portable" and "Entitled to continue after retirement or divorce" are **NOT** sufficient substitutes for the term "guaranteed renewable." If your policy is not guaranteed renewable, you may want to consider replacing it. Consistent with our recommendation throughout this book, seek the advice of an *Objective Financial Advisor* prior to canceling, replacing, or making any modifications whatsoever to a currently in-force LTC insurance policy. *(For more on the implications of insurance companies exiting the long-term care insurance market, see the Introduction to Part 3.)*

Q. *What recourse does a policyholder have if they believe they have a legitimate complaint to file against an insurer or an agent?*

A. Your best defense against a problem with an insurance company or agent is to follow our advice in *Chapter 12* about carefully choosing an insurance carrier, and our advice about working with an *Objective Financial Advisor* and the agent they recommend.

But if you purchased coverage from someone you believe has not served you ethically, or from an insurance company you believe has not treated you fairly, contact the insurance department in your state. Each state's insurance department has a formal process for filing a complaint.

Q. *Is there an insurance policy that covers "short-term care?"*

A. Yes. Short-term care insurance policies cover you for less than one year of care. In order for a policy to be called "long-term care insurance," the maximum lifetime benefit must be at least one year.

Short-term care insurance is not a good value. These policies are designed for people who can't afford LTC insurance. It's unlikely that people who can't afford LTC insurance will receive much benefit from a short-term care policy. These policies are mainly designed to help insurance agents make sales to consumers who were initially interested in LTC insurance but found the premium to be too high.

Q. *What is your opinion on the Federal LTC Insurance Program (FLTCIP)?*

A. When a new law went into effect in 2002 creating the Federal LTC Insurance Program, the federal government sent a clear signal that long-term care financing through government entitlement programs will be limited in the future.

FLTCIP is a long-term care insurance program available to federal employees, including military personnel. The program is not a guaranteed issue program; underwriting takes place with each application.

We recommend that a person who qualifies for this program ask an *Objective Financial Advisor* for a referral to an LTC Planning and Insurance expert to assist them in determining whether or not this program is a good value for their situation. In particular, it's important to thoroughly understand the implications of the "Catastrophic Coverage Limitation" clause contained in this coverage, which could limit the maximum benefits of the coverage, even if you've paid for higher benefits. In most cases, a better value can be obtained by avoiding the FLTCIP coverage and obtaining an alternate policy.

QUESTIONS ABOUT LTC INSURANCE PREMIUMS

Q. *What is a "limited-pay" LTC insurance policy?*

A. A limited-pay policy allows you to "pay up" your LTC insurance coverage in a predetermined number of years. This means that instead of paying your LTC insurance premiums for the rest of your life, you limit the number of years of payments.

Payment options for limited-pay policies are:

- Single Pay: one large premium payment
- Pay for 5 years
- Pay for 10 years
- Pay for 20 years
- Pay until age 65

There are advantages and disadvantages of choosing a limited-pay policy:

Advantages:

1. Maybe your goal is to retire in 10 years, and you would rather not make premium payments during your retirement years. Paying for coverage during your income-earning years allows you to have coverage with no out-of-pocket premium payments once the coverage is paid up. *(An example of this is explained in Chapter 11: Designing the Right Coverage: A Case Study.)*

2. If the insurance company has a rate increase after your policy is paid up, the company cannot ask you to pay additional premium. Once these policies are paid in full, they remain so for life.

3. If you purchase the inflation protection rider, the benefits of the policy continue to increase even after the policy is paid up. Your benefits continue to increase in value even though you are no longer making premium payments.

Disadvantages:

1. The premium for limited-pay policies is at least 2-3 times higher than a "pay-for-life" policy.

2. If you are not able to keep your LTC insurance policy in force because, for example, your finances change and you can no longer afford the premium, purchasing a limited pay policy would be a more costly financial mistake.

3. If you go on permanent claim during the premium payment years and the policy is placed on waiver of premium *(see Glossary),* you have paid extra premium for no gain in extra benefit.

Limited-pay policies can be a good choice for business owners who plan to retire in a predetermined number of years. In addition, business owners may benefit from tax advantages by deducting the premium as a business expense. *(This is explained in more detail in Chapter 15: Tax Advantages of Long-Term Care Insurance.)* High income earning executives, who may be in their last 5 to 20 years of employment, are also good candidates for considering limited-pay policies.

Q. *Are there ways to obtain discounts on LTC insurance premiums?*

A. Yes. You can obtain several types of discounts with the same policy. For example, most companies offer a spousal or partner discount. This discount is negligible with some companies and substantial with others. A discount of 15% to 20% is typical.

Another discount can be obtained by those in excellent health. This discount averages 15% with most companies.

But whether or not the company offers a discount, as well as the percentage of that discount, is less important than comparing coverage and premium rates among several top-rated insurance companies. One company may offer substantial discounts on a percentage basis, but the overall premium will be higher than the premium on a policy offered by an insurance company that offers lower percentage discounts.

Q. *Do LTC insurance policies have a grace period for paying the premium?*

A. By law, individually issued LTC insurance policies have a grace period of at least 31 days; the insured has up to 31 days after the due date to make sure the premium is received by the insurance company. After that period, the insurance company can terminate the policy.

Q. *Is it true that premium rates on issued policies can never be raised?*

A. This is **not** true but is a common misconception. While premium rates cannot be raised due to advancing age, deteriorating health, or claims, the carrier **can** apply for a "class-wide" rate increase that affects all policyholders who have the same policy "form" from that particular company. You can reduce your chances of having frequent premium rate increases by following the guidelines offered in *Chapter 12: Choosing the Right Insurance Carrier and Agent.* But if trends continue, premium rates will go up on all policies periodically.

Q. If an insurance company has a premium rate increase on an LTC insurance policy, does the policyholder have options other than to pay the higher premium?

A. Yes. If a rate increase is issued, the insurance company must offer the policyholder the option of reducing the policy benefits instead of paying the rate increase. This allows the policyholder to maintain the same premium rate but with reduced policy benefits.

QUESTIONS ABOUT LTC INSURANCE BENEFITS

Q. *What are the "Reduced Home Care" and "Reduced Assisted Living Facility" benefits, which are available with some comprehensive LTC insurance policies?*

A. Comprehensive LTC insurance policies pay for care in any environment: your home, an assisted living community, or a nursing home. As explained in *Chapter 10,* we recommend Comprehensive LTC Insurance as opposed to coverage that only pays for care in one environment.

Some Comprehensive LTC Insurance policies allow you to purchase a benefit amount for home care or assisted living facility care that is less than the benefit amount you purchase for nursing home care. For example, if you elect a daily benefit amount for nursing home care of $150 per day, you may be able to choose a reduced home care or assisted living facility care benefit amount of half that amount, or $75 per day. Choosing the reduced benefit will not save a significant amount on the overall premium.

We **do not** recommend choosing the reduced benefit option. Choosing this option may financially force you into a nursing home because of the low benefit amount for care in your home or an assisted living facility.

Q. *What is the "Caregiver Training" benefit of an LTC insurance policy?*

A. When a policyholder needs long-term care services, the family may want to hire someone they personally trust to assist in caring for the loved one. The "caregiver training" benefit pays for specific training that may be needed to assist the policyholder. For example, training may be provided to teach skills needed to care for a patient with Alzheimer's disease or to teach a person to use special equipment or administer medications. This benefit is included in most Comprehensive LTC Insurance policies.

Q. *What is the "Bed Reservation" benefit of an LTC insurance policy?*

A. There are times when residents of assisted living communities or nursing homes need to be hospitalized for short periods of time. When this happens, there is a chance that the resident could lose their room at the facility because the facility is not obligated to save the patient's room unless the patient pays the fee during their absence. In response to this situation, the LTC insurance industry designed the bed reservation benefit, which is included in most Comprehensive LTC Insurance policies. The benefit states that the insurance company will continue to pay for the room in the facility during the temporary absence of the policyholder. The bed reservation benefit varies by policy but usually pays benefits for 15 to 30 days per year.

Q. *If a person has minor health conditions but is issued long-term care coverage, will the insurance company pay a claim caused by one of the existing health conditions if the claim occurs immediately after the policy is issued? In other words, are there pre-existing condition clauses in LTC insurance policies?*

A. No, there are no pre-existing condition clauses. Therefore, the policy will pay benefits if a legitimate claim is submitted immediately after the policy is issued, even if the claim is the result of an existing health condition. However, you must disclose any health condition(s) at the time of application. A misrepresentation on your application could cause a claim to be denied. *It is important to answer all questions on the application correctly and thoroughly.*

Your Next Step

Congratulations on finishing a book about one of the hardest subjects to face. As a reminder, the major points of this book are:

➤ Your LTC Plan **MUST** be integrated with your financial and estate objectives. To make sure this happens, use the *Smart LTC Planning* process.

➤ **DO NOT** rely on the services of a financial professional or insurance agent who uses a non-integrative approach of simply trying to sell you insurance.

Your next steps are:

➤ An online tool available at **www.smartltcplan.com** can help you develop your own personal plan for paying for long-term care. It uses the *Smart LTC Planning* process.

➤ If you need personal assistance with developing your plan, meet with an *Objective Financial Advisor* (see page 59).

APPENDIX

ACRONYMS

AAHSA	American Association of Homes and Services for the Aging
AARP	American Association of Retired Persons
ADLs	Activities of Daily Living
BBA	Balanced Budget Act of 1997
CCAC	Continuing Care Accreditation Commission
CCRC	Continuing Care Retirement Community
CFP	Certified Financial Planner
CPA	Certified Public Accountant
DRA	Deficit Reduction Act
ERISA	Employee Retirement Income Security Act
FLTCIP	Federal Long-Term Care Insurance Program
HIPAA	Health Insurance Portability and Accountability Act
IADLs	Incidental Activities of Daily Living
LPN	Licensed Practical Nurse
LTC	Long-Term Care
NADSA	National Adult Day Services Association
NAIC	National Association of Insurance Commissioners
NCOA	National Council on Aging
NTQ	Non-Tax Qualified
OBRA	Omnibus Budget Reconciliation Act
RN	Registered Nurse
TQ	Tax-Qualified

GLOSSARY

— A —

Accelerated Benefits: A clause in a life insurance policy that allows payment of benefits for long-term care services.

Accumulation Period: The amount of time an insured is given to accumulate the number of days of care needed to satisfy the elimination period of a long-term care insurance policy.

Activities of Daily Living (ADLs): Physical functions that are performed on a daily basis, such as bathing, dressing, eating, transferring, toileting, and continence. The ability or inability to perform these functions often determines whether an individual is capable of living independently. Long-term care insurance policies assess the ability and inability to perform ADLs as criteria for determining eligibility for LTC insurance benefits.

Acute Care: Medical care received from licensed health professionals and/or hospitals with the aim of full restoration or rehabilitation of physical functions. Acute care usually refers to a treatment period of 100 days or less, which we define as short-term care.

Adult Day Center: A facility in which services and care are provided to individuals who are unable to remain at home alone during the day. These services might also include social and recreational events to alleviate the social isolation that a person living alone might experience. Caretakers who are regularly employed during the day frequently utilize these centers. Senior centers and community centers often offer adult day programs.

Adverse Selection: When there are a disproportionate number of people in an "insurance pool" who are unhealthy, resulting in a higher rate of claims than expected. Over time, usually results in the need to increase premium rates in order to cover the cost of claims.

Alzheimer's Disease: A progressive, irreversible form of dementia that causes severe intellectual deterioration that eventually results in complete dependency. It affects 5% of those over 65 and nearly half of those over 80. The cause of the disease is unknown at this time. Symptoms begin with loss of memory and rational thinking, with progressive deterioration over the course of several years.

Ambulatory: Able to move about, generally without any type of assistance.

Ambulatory with Assistance: Able to move about with the aid of a cane, crutch, brace, wheelchair, or walker.

Ancillary Services: Personal care services such as podiatry, dentistry, and hair care that are needed by a nursing home or assisted living resident but are not typically included in the basic fees charged by the facility.

Assisted Living Facility/Community: A residential facility for those who may need help with activities of daily living or supervision due to cognitive impairment. These facilities usually include private units (apartments or rooms), two to three meals a day, laundry services, transportation, activities, and housekeeping. In most facilities, a 24-hour staff is available to meet residents' needs.

— **B** —

Bed Reservation Benefit: A covered expense in most long-term care insurance policies that allows a facility to receive payment for a bed being held for a resident who requires temporary hospitalization.

Benefit Amount: A set dollar amount of benefit per day, week, or month that a long-term care insurance policy will pay for long-term care costs.

Benefit Period Maximum: The maximum amount a long-term care insurance policy will pay for covered services in a lifetime. The benefit can be expressed in length of time or a dollar amount. This benefit may be payable to the owner of the policy or to a third party, such as a facility or home care provider.

Benefit Triggers: The criteria used by insurance carriers to determine eligibility for long-term care insurance benefits. The best policies "trigger" benefits when a policyholder is unable to perform two or more ADLs without assistance **or** when cognitive impairment is determined to be severe enough for the person to need supervision.

Board and Care Homes: "Homes" that provide limited supervision and care to their residents. Medical personnel are usually not on staff and the administration of medications is usually not available.

Bundled Policies: Policies that "bundle" life insurance or some other financial product with long-term care insurance.

— **C** —

Care Coordination: Assistance with the development and implementation of the plan of care including helping to identify appropriate services and making arrangements to receive care.

Caregiver: A person giving assistance to another. Assistance is usually required due to medical reasons, inability to perform activities of daily living, or cognitive impairment.

Caregiver Training Benefit: A benefit in a long-term care insurance policy that pays for someone to learn the best methods to use in caring for the policyholder who is on claim.

Chronic Illness: An illness characterized by permanency and/or residual disability requiring a long period of care.

Cognitive Impairment: Deficiency in short or long-term memory; orientation as to person, place, and time; abstract reasoning; or judgment as it relates to safety awareness.

Coinsurance: The process of paying for a portion of the cost of care out of pocket.

Community-Based Services: Services designed to help older people stay independent and in their own homes for as long as possible.

Comprehensive Long-Term Care Insurance Policy: A long-term care insurance policy that covers care in any environment, including facility care and home care.

Conditionally Renewable: A policy that may be canceled at any time for various reasons, including excessive claims history. No longer allowed in currently issued long-term care insurance policies, but older in-force policies may contain this clause.

Conservator: If a court determines that a person is unable to manage his/her property and funds for some reason, either physical or mental, a "conservator" may be appointed by the court to properly manage the property and funds for that person.

Continuing Care Retirement Community (CCRC): Also called "Life Care Communities," these communities offer the full spectrum of living and care arrangements—from independent living to nursing home care—all within the same community.

Custodial Care: Care to help an individual perform their activities of daily living, such as bathing, dressing, and eating.

— D —

Dementia. Deterioration of cognitive faculties.

— E —

Elimination Period: Also known as the "deductible," the time period during which a policyholder pays for covered services before a long-term care insurance policy will begin to pay for those services.

Estate Recovery: When a Medicaid recipient dies and leaves an estate, Medicaid may seek to recover from the estate the money it spent on care for the recipient by using the Estate Recovery process.

Estate Planning: Addresses tax-efficient ways to acquire, preserve, and transfer a person's financial wealth to other parties, both during and after life.

— F —

Facility Care Only Policy: A long-term care insurance policy that only covers care in a facility, such as a nursing home or assisted living community. Home care is not covered by these policies.

Facility Certification: A certificate given to a facility that is in compliance with a set of federal standards regarding staffing, cleanliness, and maintenance of records. Nursing homes must be certified before they are reimbursed for care provided to Medicaid recipients.

Financial Planning: The overall process of setting financial goals, evaluating where you are with respect to those goals, laying out a plan to achieve them, implementing the plan, and modifying the plan as your current situation and goals change.

Formal Care Provider: Caregivers who are trained specialists and provide long-term care services as a career.

Free-Look Period: Also called the "Right to Return" provision. A newly insured long-term care insurance policyholder has the right to return the policy to the company within 30 days of receiving it, for a full refund of any deposits or premium payments paid.

— **G** —

Grace Period: A length of time after the premium due date during which the coverage remains in force even though the premium payment has not been paid. This period is normally 31 days.

Group Long-Term Care Insurance: Coverage offered by employers or other groups that is normally issued on a "guaranteed issue" or "modified guaranteed issue" basis. This means that the applicant could be accepted for coverage without full underwriting.

Guaranteed Issue: A policy issued without any underwriting requirements. Coverage may be obtained regardless of current or past health conditions.

Guaranteed Purchase Option: A provision giving the insured the right to purchase additional coverage at set intervals without having to reapply and health-qualify for coverage. The premium for the additional coverage will be based on the policyholder's age at the time of benefit increase.

Guaranteed Renewable: A policy that can only be canceled because of non-payment of premium. Adjustments in premium may be made, but only for a whole class of insureds and not just the individual.

— **H** —

Health Insurance Portability and Accountability Act (HIPAA): Legislation inacted in 1997 that resulted in the standardization of long-term care insurance policies and clarified the tax treatment of benefits and premiums for long-term care insurance.

Home Care: Personal care services provided by trained but non-skilled personnel. Does not require the supervision of a physician.

Home Care Only Policy: A policy that does not cover care in any type of facility. Typically covers home health care, home care, and some homemaker services.

Home Health Agency: A private or public agency that specializes in providing skilled nurses, homemakers, home health aides, and therapeutic services (e.g., physical therapy) in an individual's home.

Home Health Care: Care or services received from skilled personnel in your home. The treatment or plan of care is supervised by a physician or registered nurse.

Hospice Care: A special way of caring for a terminally ill patient and emotionally supporting his or her family. This care addresses physical, spiritual, emotional, psychological, social, financial, and legal needs while enhancing the dying person's quality of life.

— I —

Incidental Activities of Daily Living (IADLs): Activities such as cooking, cleaning, shopping, laundry, managing money, administering medications, and providing transportation.

Inflation Protection Rider: An option on a long-term care insurance policy that provides for automatic increases in benefit levels to hedge against inflationary increases in long-term care service costs.

Informal Caregivers: Caregivers who care for a patient out of love or a sense of duty rather than as a profession.

Institutionalization: To admit a person into a facility, such as a nursing home, where they will usually have an extended or indefinite stay.

Intermediate Care: Care provided when recovery and rehabilitation are the primary goals and 24-hour-a-day physician supervision is not needed.

— L —

Lapse: Termination of a policy when a premium is not paid.

Life Care Arrangement or Life Care Contract: A financial arrangement typically utilized by Continuing Care Retirement Communities. The resident pays an initial lump sum when they move in and a predetermined monthly amount thereafter.

Lifetime Policy: A long-term care insurance policy in which there is no maximum limit to the cumulative benefits that can be collected.

Lifetime Maximum Benefit: The total dollar amount that can be collected from a long-term care insurance policy. Choices in the lifetime maximum range from as short as one year to unlimited coverage, which has no cumulative dollar or time limit.

Limited Pay: Long-term care insurance policies in which premiums are paid for a limited time period instead of over the life of the policy. Common periods include single payment, five-year pay, ten-year pay, and twenty-year pay.

Long-Term Care: Medical and social care given to individuals with a chronic illness, disability, or cognitive disorder. Defined by the author as needing assistance for longer than 100 days. This care may take place in a skilled nursing facility, assisted living community, adult day center, the home of the person receiving care, or someone else's home. Care can be administered by medical professionals or nonprofessional personnel.

Long-Term Care Plan: The result of the process of deliberately choosing the most appropriate resources to pay for long-term care **in advance** of the need for care. The plan should be in writing and a copy provided to family members and financial advisors.

— **M** —

Meals on Wheels: A program that delivers meals to people who are homebound.

Medicaid: A welfare program administered by the federal and individual state governments that helps pay for certain types of medical care given to needy and low-income people. A nursing home must be certified by Medicaid in order to be reimbursed for care provided to a Medicaid recipient.

Medi-Cal: The Medicaid program in California.

Medicare: A federal health insurance program that pays for health care for people over 65 and some people under 65 who are disabled. Part A is hospital insurance and Part B is medical insurance. Medicare pays for limited short-term care in a skilled nursing facility but only under certain conditions. Medicare **DOES NOT** pay for long-term care.

Medicare Supplement Insurance: Private insurance policies that cover health care costs not fully covered by Medicare. Medicare Supplement insurance **DOES NOT** pay for long-term care.

Medigap Insurance: Another name for Medicare Supplement insurance.

Modified Guaranteed Issue: People who are in poor health but can certify that they are currently not needing long-term care services, or do not have a condition that will result in the need for long-term care in the near future, may qualify for coverage under this type of issue.

— **N** —

National Association of Insurance Commissioners (NAIC): A membership organization of state insurance commissioners. One of its goals is to promote uniformity of state regulation and legislation related to insurance.

Nonforfeiture Benefit: Usually available as an option, it allows the policyholder to receive some type of benefit if the policy lapses. The benefit is usually in the form of a paid-up maximum benefit equal to the cumulative premiums paid at the time of the lapse.

Non-integrated Approach: Addressing one aspect of insurance or financial planning in a vacuum instead of considering all aspects within the context of the overall personal and financial situation, and the objectives of the individual or family.

Non-Tax-Qualified Policies (NTQ): Policies that do not conform to HIPAA's requirements and do not receive the same favorable tax treatment as Tax-Qualified policies.

Nursing Home: A licensed facility that provides general nursing care to those who are chronically ill or unable to take care of daily living needs.

— **O** —

Objective Financial Advisor: Financial advisors with the following attributes: Seek long-term relationships with their clients; no agenda for advising you to buy or invest in certain financial products; have a transparent and easy to understand compensation model; do not accept commissions, referral fees, or kickbacks; A willingness to assist with psychology of money issues.

Outline of Coverage: A description of the coverage and benefits of a long-term care insurance policy. Includes a statement of exclusions; limitations in the policy; a statement of the terms under which the policy may be returned and the premiums refunded; and a description of the policy benefits.

— **P** —

Partnership Policy: A type of policy that allows you to protect some of your assets if you apply for Medicaid after exhausting your policy's benefits. Currently available in some states.

Plan of Care: An organized schedule of treatment or care for a patient, usually developed by care coordinators, physicians, nurses, or hospital discharge planners.

Planning Gap: A shortfall between the resources allocated to meet long-term care costs and the estimated cost of that care.

Power of Attorney: A written agreement that authorizes a relative, attorney, business associate, friend, or another person to sign documents and enter into transactions on behalf of the individual.

— **R** —

Respite Care: The in-home care given to a chronically ill beneficiary in order to give the regular caregiver(s) a break.

Restoration of Benefits Rider: If you elect this rider when you buy a policy with less than an "Unlimited Benefit Maximum," and you use a portion of your policy benefits, the entire pool of benefits in the policy will be restored if your health returns and you go without care for a specified period of time.

— **S** —

Sandwich Generation: Families that are raising children and caring for aging parent(s) at the same time.

Senility: Mental deterioration that sometimes accompanies aging.

Senior Center: A community-based facility that provides seniors with recreation, education, cultural enrichment, and social events.

Short-Term Care: Care that is required for less than 100 days.

Skilled Care: Care provided by a trained medical person and under the supervision of a doctor or other qualified medical professional.

Skilled Nursing Facility (SNF): A facility providing skilled care by licensed staff.

***Smart LTC Plan*™:** The result of a 7-step process for choosing your most appropriate option for paying for long-term care. Developed within the context of your personal and financial objectives.

Sponsored Long-Term Care Insurance: Offered by an employer or other "group." Unlike true group insurance, however, sponsored programs use the same strict underwriting guidelines as individually issued policies.

Spousal or Partner Discount: If a husband and wife or partners purchase coverage from the same insurance carrier, they may receive a premium discount on both policies.

Survivorship Benefit: Offered as a rider, this provision states that if one spouse dies after paying premiums for a certain period of time, the living spouse is no longer required to pay premiums on their own policy. Requires both spouses to have coverage with the same insurer and normally requires that both insureds go claim-free for a certain number of years.

— **T** —

Tax-Qualified Policies (TQ): Long-term care insurance policies created by HIPAA legislation in 1996. Resulted in the standardization of long-term care insurance policies and the clarification of the tax consequences of receiving benefits.

Third Party Notification of Lapse: Requires insurers to send a notice to an individual designated by the insured before a policy is canceled due to non-payment of premium.

—— **U** ——

Underwriting: The process of examining, accepting, or rejecting insurance risks, and classifying those accepted to charge the appropriate premium for each.

Uninsurable: Individuals who are not eligible for insurance due to the presence of a health condition that requires them to already receive care, or who may have a higher probability of needing care in the future. Examples would be people who have already been diagnosed with Alzheimer's disease or Parkinson's disease.

—— **W** ——

Waiver of Premium: A provision in some LTC insurance policies that states the insured is not required to continue paying premiums while he or she is on claim.

REFERENCES

American Health Care Association. 2004. News release: "New BDO Seidman Analysis of Nation's Medicaid Program," February 4. Available as a download from **www.ahca.org.**

Congressional Budget Office. 2000. "Options to Expand Federal Health, Retirement, and Education Activities," *CBO Memorandum,* June. Prepared by the Health and Human Resources Division. Available as a pdf download from **www.cbo.gov.**

Douglas, Jennifer. 2001. *Long-Term Care Insurance: Trends and Outlook,* LIMRA International.

Employee Benefits Research Institute (EBRI). 2004. "Will Americans Ever Become Savers?" *The 14th Retirement Confidence Survey,* April. Retrieved from **www.ebri.org.**

Harper, Sarah. 2004. "Aging Society," *The Oxford Magazine,* March.

Hayes, Robert D., Nancy G. Boyd, and Kenneth W. Hollman. 1999. "What Attorneys Should Know About Long-Term Care Insurance," *The Elder Law Journal,* Vol. 7, No. 1.

Health Care Financing Administration (see The Centers for Medicare and Medicaid Services). **www.cms.hhs.gov.**

Health Insurance Association of America (HIAA). 2001. "Who Buys Long-Term Care Insurance in the Workplace?" October. Available as a download from **www.hiaa.org.**

Hewitt Associates. 2004. Press release: "Hewitt Study Shows U.S. Employees Sluggish in Interacting with 401(k) Plans," May 24.

Journal of Financial Planning, February 2001. "Coming of Age: The Shifting Dynamics of Elder Care" by Jacqueline M. Quinn.

Long-Term Care Financing Strategy Group. 2004. "A Vast Majority of Americans Over Age 45 Unprotected Against the Risk of Needing Long-Term Care, According to Second Annual Study." From *The Index of Long-Term Care Uninsured,* Washington, D.C., May 17.

LTCi Sales Strategies. Vol. 3, No. 2. Reprinted with permission. Available through **www.LTCSales.com.**

Merlis, Mark. 2003. Medical Expenditures Panel Survey cited in "Private Long-Term Care Insurance: Who Should Buy It and What Should They Buy?" March. Available as a download from **www.kff.org.**

Metropolitan Life Insurance Company. 2004. Press release: "Caring for an Aging Loved One at a Distance Costs Much in Time, Money, and Hours on the Job," MetLife Mature Market Institute.

Metropolitan Life Insurance Study. 1999. "The MetLife Juggling Act Study: Balancing Caregiving with Work and the Costs Involved," November. Available as a download from **www.metlife.com** (search Mature Market Institute for pdf report).

Metropolitan Life Insurance Study. 2001. "The MetLife Study of Employed Caregivers: Does Long-Term Care Insurance Make a Difference?" Findings from a national study by the National Alliance for Caregiving and LifePlans, Inc., March. Available as a download from **www.metlife.com** (search Mature Market Institute for pdf report).

National Alliance for Caregiving and AARP. 2004. "Caregiving in the U.S." Funded by the MetLife Foundation. Available as a download from **www.caregiving.org.**

National Association of Insurance Commissioners, **www.naic.org.**

National Council on Aging. Definition of "senior center" by the National Institute of Senior Centers. Retrieved from **www.ncoa.org.**

National Council on the Aging. 1999. "Americans Look to Employers and Government for Help with Long-Term Care," March 23.

O'Neil, John. 2004. "Easing the Burdens of Care." *The New York Times,* May 11. Available for purchase from **www.nytimes.com.**

Parker-Pope, Tara. 2004. "Health Matters," *The Wall Street Journal,* June 28.

Prenda, Kimberly M. and Margie E. Lachman. 2001. "Planning for the Future: A Life Management Strategy," *Psychology and Aging,* Vol. 16, No. 2, pp. 206-216.

Rush University Medical Center. 2004. "Diabetics at Significantly Higher Risk for Alzheimer's Disease," May 17. Available as a download from **www.rush.edu.**

Slome, Jesse R. 2002. Paraphrased interview reprinted with permission from *Long-Term Care Insurance Sales Strategies,* Vol. 4, No. 4. **www.LTCSales.com**

U.S. Department of Health and Human Services. 2003a. "A Profile of Older Americans: 2003," *Administration on Aging.* Retrieved from **www.aoa.gov.**

U.S. Department of Health and Human Services. 2003b. "Family Caregivers: Our Heroes on the Frontlines of Long-Term Care," December 16. Retrieved from **www.hhs.gov.**

U.S. Department of Health and Human Services. 2005. *Medicare and You 2005.* Available as a download from **www.medicare.gov/publications/pubs/pdf/10050. pdf.**

U.S. Department of Labor. 2001. *Report of the Working Group on Long-Term Care,* November 14. Retrieved from **www.dol.gov.**

U.S. General Accounting Office. 2001. "Baby Boom Generation Increases Challenge of Financing Needed Services," Statement of William J. Scanlon, Director, Health Care Issues, GAO Report No. GAO-01-563T, March 27. Available as a download from **www.gao.gov.**

University of California. The Institute for Health and Aging. Retrieved from **www.nurseweb.ucsf.edu.**

University of Pittsburgh Medical Center. 2004. Press release: "University of Pittsburgh Finds That People Would Trade Longevity for Quality End-of-Life Care," May 19. Retrieved from **www.eurekalert.org.**

Willingness to Assist with "Psychology of Money" Issues; Steve Merrell; **www.smarteggnest.com**

RESOURCES

Administration on Aging: **www.aoa.gov**

Alternatives for Seniors: **www.alternativesforseniors.com**

Alzheimer's Association: **www.alz.org**

Leading Age: **www.leadingage.org**

Assisted Living Federation of America: **www.alfa.org**

Caregiving: **www.caring.com**

Center for Long-Term Care Reform, Inc.: **www.centerltc.com**

Family Caregiver Alliance: **www.caregiver.org**

Health in Aging: **www.healthinaging.org**

Medicare: **www.medicare.gov**

National Adult Day Services Association: **www.nadsa.org**

National Association for Home Care: **www.nahc.org**

National Family Caregivers Association: **www.nfcacares.org**

National Senior Citizen's Law Center: **www.nsclc.org**

Superior LTC Planning Services, Inc.: **www.superiorltc.com**

Visiting Nurse Associations of America: **www.vnaa.org**

CHARTS & GRAPHS

INDEX

A

Activities of Daily Living (ADLs), 1, 13, 21, 23, 25, 29, 34, 35, 44, 48, 50, 90, 137-138, 145, 185, 187-189, 191

Adult day centers, 22-23, 102

Adverse selection, 75, 165-166, 168-169, 187

Alzheimer's Association, 29, 200

Alzheimer's disease, 5, 14, 16, 20, 25-26, 29, 32, 35, 90, 106, 112, 117, 119, 138, 181, 187, 195, 198

American Association of Homes and Services for the Aging (AAHSA), 185

American Association of Retired Persons (AARP), 28, 42, 185, 198

American Health Care Association, 30, 197

Assisted living communities, 20, 25-29, 32, 34-35, 40, 52, 102, 120, 181

Assisted Living Federation of America, 25, 200

Automatic inflation protection benefit, 107-108, 110, 118, 121-122

B

Bed reservation benefit, 181, 188

Board and care homes, 24-25, 32, 102, 188

C

Care coordination, 96-97, 138, 140-145, 160, 188

Care coordinator, 140, 142-144

Care manager, 140, 143

Caregiver training benefit, 181, 188

Cash method, 101, 113

C Corporations, 154, 164

Chronic condition, 20

Cognitive impairment, 48, 50, 134, 137-138, 188-189

Coinsuring, 95, 107

Comprehensive long-term care insurance policies, 102

Continuing Care Accreditation Commission (CCAC), 29, 185

Continuing Care Retirement Communities (CCRC), 27-29, 32, 47, 185, 189

CPA, 96, 122, 185

Custodial care, 6, 13, 19-20, 32, 48, 189

N

National Adult Day Services Association (NADSA), 23, 185, 200

National Aging Services Network, 24

National Council on Aging (NCOA), 23, 60, 82, 185, 198

New York State Partnership Program, 88

Non-cancelable LTC insurance, 174

Non-integrated Approach, 1, 65, 70, 87, 116, 120-121, 123, 164, 167-168, 193, 201

Non-skilled care, 19-20, 32

Non-tax-qualified policies (NTQ), 152, 185, 193

O

Objective Financial Advisor(s)™, 1, 38, 55, 57, 59-67, 69, 87, 96, 99, 115-116, 123, 125, 130, 133, 140, 153, 155, 161, 163-164, 166-169, 174-177, 182, 193

P

Parkinson's disease, 7, 16, 68, 90, 195

Partnership programs, 93, 149, 160-162

Personal care, 22-24, 36, 51, 81, 187, 190

Personal tolerance for risk, 62, 69, 95, 104-105, 107, 115-117, 120, 124

Plan of care, 138, 141-143, 188, 191, 193

Pre-existing [health] condition, 182

Preferred premium rate, 104, 116

R

Reciprocity, 160

Reimbursement method, 100-101, 113

Restoration of benefits, 109, 194

Retirement planning, 62

Riders, 107-108, 113

Risk management, 60, 62, 88-89

Risk pool, 130

Robert Wood Johnson Foundation, 102, 159